CLINICAL LEGAL EDUCATION

A TEXTBOOK FOR LAW SCHOOL CLINICAL PROGRAMS

DAVID F. CHAVKIN

Professor of Law
American University
Washington College of Law

ISBN#: 1-4224-0725-X

Editorial Offices
744 Broad Street, Newark, NJ 07102 (973) 820-2000
201 Mission St., San Francisco, CA 94105-1831 (415) 908-3200
701 East Water Street, Charlottesville, VA 22902-7587 (434) 972-7600
www.lexis.com

(Pub.3612)

Dedications

This book is dedicated to:

My parents, Herbert and Shirley, who taught me many of the principles reflected in my work as a teacher;

My daughter, Rachel, who taught me (admittedly, sometimes with limited success) to temper the application of those principles with humor and sensitivity; and, most of all,

My partner, Linda, who was there at the creation of this project and supported (and occasionally drove me) through the development of this textbook.

David F. Chavkin

April 1, 2002

Table of Contents

Acknowledgments

This textbook would not have been possible without the work of and support by:

My clinical colleagues at the American University, Washington College of Law, especially Ann Shalleck, Elliott Milstein, Bob Dinerstein, Binny Miller, Rick Wilson, Susan Bennett, and Nancy Polikoff, who welcomed me to clinical legal education; encouraged me to question, research, and write; and nurtured that process of ongoing exploration through their feedback and patience.

Dean Claudio Grossman of the Washington College of Law, American University, and Associate Deans Bob Dinerstein and Andy Pike who supported this project financially and spiritually and helped create an atmosphere in which this kind of work could move forward.

My dean's fellows, especially Michelle Duluc and Kerry Brainard, who demonstrated commitment, creativity, and independence in conducting much of the research supporting this text.

Anderson Publishing Company and its editors, who recognized the need for a textbook to use in law school clinical programs and who supported this project through its realization.

Gary Bellow and Bea Moulton, whose groundbreaking textbook in 1978, THE LAWYERING PROCESS, MATERIALS FOR CLINICAL INSTRUCTION IN ADVOCACY, helped establish a foundation for the critical reflection and scholarship that would mark the development of clinical legal education.

David Binder and Susan Price for their text LEGAL INTERVIEWING AND COUNSELING and David Binder, Paul Bergman, and Susan Price for their text LAWYERS AS COUNSELORS for developing much of the theory for what we now know as client-centered representation; and David Binder and Paul Bergman for their text FACT INVESTIGATION and the approaches to fact analysis reflected in this text as well. Their influence on my education as a clinical teacher is sufficiently pervasive that some of their insights are doubtless reflected in this text.

Robert Bastress and Joseph Harbaugh for their text INTERVIEWING, COUNSELING, AND NEGOTIATING and their efforts to integrate the teaching of lawyering skills. Their influence is also doubtless reflected in this textbook. The bargaining chart in the chapter on "Negotiation" explicitly incorporates the chart from Joe's negotiating training materials, also reflected in the "Weber" problem that runs through the Bastress and Harbaugh text.

My co-teachers and former clinical colleagues at the University of Maryland (especially Rick North and Mary Helen McNeal), Georgetown University (especially Randi Mandelbaum), and the Catholic University of America (especially Ellen Scully and Sandy Ogilvy), and American University (especially Brenda Smith and Kate Bunker) who generously shared their ideas and their insights about clinical teaching.

The clinical teachers throughout the Mid-Atlantic region who participated in the Mid-Atlantic Clinical Theory and Practice Workshop at which a draft of this book was presented and whose comments helped reshape this text.

And, finally, my students in the various clinical courses I have taught since 1990, especially Ben Sigel, whose contributions to my education certainly exceeded anything that I could have contributed to theirs.

David F. Chavkin

April 1, 2002

Chapter 1

Introduction to
Clinical Legal Education

Welcome.

You are about to begin an educational adventure unlike anything you have previously encountered in law school. Whatever your prior experiences in law school—good, bad, or indifferent—in all of those classes you have primarily self-identified and been identified as a (law) *student*.

By contrast, in your clinic work you are about to try on for the first time the identity of *lawyer*. Although your education will still be the paramount goal throughout your clinic experience, for the first time you will be professionally responsible for the services you provide on behalf of clients and clients will be relying on you to fulfill those professional responsibilities with distinction. We hope you will find this to be both an exciting and a daunting prospect.

A. Theory and Practice

Clinical legal education reflects a marriage of theory and practice—an opportunity to "lawyer," but also to reflect on the theory and process of lawyering. In 1983, Donald Schön coined the term "reflective practicum" to refer to an educational setting in which "students mainly learn by doing, with the help of coaching." As described by Schön, the practicum is "reflective" in two senses: "it is intended to help students become proficient in a kind of reflection-in-action; and, when it works well, it involves a dialogue of coach and student that takes the form of reciprocal reflection-in-action."

This image of "coach" and "student" has both its strengths and its limitations. It correctly presents a vision in which the "coach" can help the student prepare to perform (ordinarily through work outside the sight of an audience), but one in which the student is the "player." The student is the one on the field (whether in a litigation, transactional, or other setting), the one who must ultimately demonstrate competency in the lawyering skills and values necessary for effective and responsible lawyering.

However, the image is also limited in that it ignores the numerous other teachers in the clinical process—clients, opposing parties, opposing lawyers, court personnel, and others—who will provide valuable learning opportunities and insights on a daily basis. You will learn from their verbal and non-verbal responses to you, from their reactions to your performance of lawyering tasks, and from the ways that you and your clients are treated within the legal system.

The image of a "coach" also overstates the extent to which clinical supervisors actually direct students. The process, as we shall see, is far more one of assisting, rather than directing, students in discovering the best ways to approach particular lawyering tasks and in helping students reflect on their experiences and the lessons to be drawn from them. Rather than "calling plays" for you to "run," together with your supervisor you will be identifying and sorting through options to evaluate with your clients and courses of action to implement.

So, with awareness of these strengths and limitations for the "reflective practicum" model, we will work to create a setting in which you will feel free to talk about your experiences, your decisions, your actions, and, sometimes, your mistakes.

B. Skills and Values

Clinical legal education reflects a marriage of lawyering skills and values. Standard 301(a) of the American Bar Association Standards for Approval of Law Schools defines the objectives for the "Program of Legal Education" (the course of study) at American law schools. The current version of this standard provides as follows:

> A law school shall maintain an educational program that prepares
> its graduates for admission to the bar and to participate effectively
> and responsibly in the legal profession.

The language "participate effectively and responsibly" reflects a requirement that legal education transmit both the *skills* that will allow graduates to practice law effectively and also the *values* that will allow graduates to practice law responsibly.

The notion that law schools have the responsibility to teach "skills" and "values" to law students is a relatively recent development in American legal education. It is in large part attributable to the issuance of the MacCrate Task Force Report in 1992.

In 1989, the Section of Legal Education and Admission to the Bar of the American Bar Association established the *Task Force on Law Schools and the Profession: Narrowing the Gap* to examine the extent to which law schools were actually preparing students for the profession. The Task Force was chaired by Robert MacCrate, a senior counsel with the law firm of Sullivan & Cromwell, an ABA Medal of Honor recipient, and the ABA President in 1987-88. In part because of his renown, the project came to be known informally as the MacCrate Task Force. The Task Force report, titled *Legal Education and Professional Development: An Educational Continuum*, came to be known widely as the MacCrate Report.

The MacCrate Report concluded that education in lawyering skills and professional values should be central to the mission of law schools. The Report emphasized that

> the most significant development in legal education in the post-World II era has been the growth of skills training curriculum. . . . Today, clinical courses . . . occupy an important place in the curriculum of virtually all ABA-approved law schools.

We will also emphasize the importance of lawyering skills and values throughout your clinical experience. However, because skills and values are so interrelated, we will often depart from the dichotomy between skills and values reflected in the MacCrate Report. Instead, you will frequently find the two concepts merged together here as *lawyeringskillsandvalues*.

After the issuance of the MacCrate Report, a conference was held to consider the implications of the Report. Former ABA President Talbot "Sandy" D'Alemberte delivered a speech at the conference that was characterized as having "unleashed a thunderbolt criticizing the direction [legal education] is taking in the United States." D'Alemberte, a former dean at Florida State University College of Law and later president of that University, criticized the failure of law schools to teach students to be lawyers.

Throughout your legal education, you have probably been told that legal education is designed to teach you to "think like a lawyer." D'Alemberte described that viewpoint as a "damn strange statement." He continued his criticism by questioning, "What would you say to . . . educators in other fields if they said, 'We don't teach you to be a musician, actor, historian, physicist— but only to think like one?'" D'Alemberte also criticized the impact of inadequate skills training in forcing students to choose such jobs as law firm associates because they are not qualified to practice law on graduation.

C. Experiential Learning

Clinical legal education both anticipated and reflected the changes in the ABA accreditation standards and the issuance and implementation of the MacCrate Report. The role of experiential learning in developing skills and values required for responsible and effective lawyering dates back in the United States to at least the early 1930s. In 1933, Jerome Frank wrote a seminal article that would become almost a blueprint for clinical educators thirty-five years later. In that article, Frank explained that clinical education helps students see the human side of the administration of justice, including: how juries decide cases; the uncertain character of the "facts" of a case; how legal rights often turn on the faulty memory, bias, or perjury of a witness; the effects of fatigue, alertness, political pull, graft, laziness, conscientiousness, patience, impatience, prejudice, and open-mindedness of judges; the methods of negotiating contracts and settlements; and the nature of draftsmanship.

Frank's theoretical analysis took life in the late 1960s when CLEPR (the Council on Legal Education for Professional Responsibility) provided the financial impetus clinical legal education needed to take root in American legal education. The Ford Foundation created CLEPR, with a grant in excess of $10 million, to "jumpstart" the creation of clinical programs at many law schools. Through the vision of CLEPR's President, Bill Pincus, CLEPR provided more than 100 grants to law schools to provide lawyer-client experiences for their students. Most of these schools then continued and expanded these programs started with CLEPR grants.

The development of these programs was furthered by the involvement of former public defenders and legal aid/legal services attorneys in these clinical programs. Many of these public interest lawyers brought with them to legal education a healthy skepticism of law school academic programs and a desire to develop new theories for educating responsible and effective lawyers. These clinical teachers also looked very different from the professors who had taught them in law school; there were more women and more minorities among them and they brought experiences in practice that were often lacking (and sometimes devalued) in law school faculties.

D. The Current Landscape

Today there are three major types of experiential learning on display in American law schools. These three forms of experiential learning are simulations, externships and in-house clinics. In simulation courses, students are given the opportunity to learn about lawyering skills and values in a simulated context—usually a fictitious case based on a real-life case file. In externship (or internship) courses, students are given the opportunity to work in a legal setting (often in a government agency or with a non-profit legal services provider or a judge) and to perform some legal tasks (usually legal research and fact investigation and legal writing) while observing "real" lawyers in action.

While simulation courses and externship courses can provide students with the opportunity to gain necessary skills and values and to learn about the kind of lawyer they may want to be in practice, these courses are necessarily limited in their benefits. Simulations are, by their nature, artificial and students will never engage in the same way they would in a real-life case. Externships are, by their nature, limited in scope because students are working for lawyers and judges and are not actually assuming the roles of lawyer or judge.

This textbook focuses on the third model of experiential learning—in-house clinical legal education. As we will see in our discussion of clinical methodology, it is an educational model built on the concept of "learning by doing" with supervision provided by clinical teachers, professors committed first and foremost to the education of you, our students.

As you have probably already noticed, this textbook uses the words "we" and "our" to refer to the educational process in which we are engaged. This terminology represents a purposeful choice of words. Unlike traditional classroom courses, the clinical experience is largely collaborative. You will be collaborating with your clinical teachers in ways that are very different from even the small seminars that you may have taken in law school. You will be collaborating with administrative staff in the clinic and with other clinic students. From this joint enterprise in learning, we hope together to provide you with many opportunities from which to learn about your future profession and about yourself.

Chapter 2
Clinical Methodology

As we have discussed, clinical legal education has pedagogical goals that differ from those in non-clinical courses. In order to achieve these unique goals, special teaching methods have been developed to maximize the opportunities for learning throughout your clinical experience. While the opportunity to work with real-life clients to address real-world problems under the "supervision" of a trained faculty member is at the heart of the clinical experience, clinical education also uses other techniques to help you develop as a reflective practitioner.

A. The Problem of the Kitchen Organizer

At its best, clinical methodology is subtle and often invisible. For that reason, we will start our discussion of clinical methodology indirectly.

Think back to the first time that you lived alone. Perhaps it occurred during your undergraduate education; perhaps it happened earlier or later in your life. One of your first tasks was to organize your kitchen—to decide where to place the dishes, the glasses, the pots and pans, and the silverware. And, imagine that a Professor of "Kitchen Organizing" was present as you began to unload your boxes. Several courses of action were available to the Professor.

First, the Professor could have told you to unpack your clothes in the bedroom while s/he unpacked your kitchen supplies. S/he would then have placed your items on the shelves based on well-established principles of "kitchen organization"—principles with which you would have had no familiarity.

The result would have been a well-organized kitchen. However, you would have learned nothing about the relevant theories of kitchen organizing and, because you had not "bought into" the theories reflected in the professor's system, it is unlikely that you would have maintained the kitchen using that model.

Second, the professor could have asked you to be present while s/he organized the kitchen. You could have interacted with the professor as s/he

7

placed items on the shelves and in drawers—asking questions as appropriate—and perhaps you might even have placed a glass or plate or fork as directed. Similar to a well-designed externship, you might have learned some of the principles of good "kitchen organizing" and you would have learned something of the work of the professional "kitchen organizer."

A well-organized kitchen would also have been produced. However, you would not have "owned" your experience as a kitchen organizer and would not have internalized the principles of kitchen organizing in the same way as when you "own" your learning process. Moreover, the kitchen might have been organized in a manner appropriate for the professor, but not necessarily for you and your intended uses of the kitchen.

Third, the professor could have taken out a blackboard and lectured on the principles of kitchen organizing. You might have had an opportunity to ask questions, although your lack of personal experience in kitchen organizing would have limited your ability to design effective questions and the lack of factual context would have limited the utility of the lecture. The professor would then have departed and you would have attempted to design an effective kitchen based on the abstract principles you had heard in the lecture.

This educational model, generally referred to as "exposition-application," is the model commonly used throughout law school (and has some role even in clinic). *To the extent* that you were able to understand the principles expounded in the lecture and *to the extent* that you were able to apply those principles in a specific factual context (your own kitchen), the result would have been a grounding in the principles of kitchen organization, an ability to apply them in context, and an effectively-organized kitchen. However, the inclusion of the words "to the extent" highlights the problems in translating the theory presented in lecture materials into the practical ability to apply that knowledge.

Fourth, the professor could have gone out to lunch and left you to organize the kitchen. You *might* have conducted research into the principles of kitchen organizing and you *might* have been successful in researching those principles. You *might* have asked yourself critical questions about your intended use of the kitchen, the locations of fixed kitchen appliances, and the kitchenware to distribute and you *might* have been successful in applying the principles you learned through research to the facts you gained through answering your questions. However, you would not have had anyone with whom to reflect on the process of research and application. And, the results, emphasized by the word "might," would have been very hit or miss.

Finally, the professor could have taken a very different role. S/he could have first sat down with you in the kitchen and talked with you about the task of organizing a kitchen. S/he would have asked you a series of questions to help you identify the issues you would have to confront in the process of organization. S/he would have asked you questions to help you think about the relevant facts about kitchen uses and equipment you would have to identify and consider and the principles you would have to learn to design an efficient and effective kitchen. Through these questions you would have begun to grapple with the specific considerations necessary to design this particular kitchen for this particular user (you) in light of your intended uses.

S/he would then have stepped back to let you begin the process and might have observed your work at particular intervals. S/he would also have met with you periodically to ask questions and to help you focus on particular aspects of the process. After the process was completed, the professor would then have helped you reflect on the steps you had undertaken to investigate, research, and implement and to help you identify principles you had developed, choices you had made, and consequences you had experienced or were likely to experience from those choices.

Like some of the other options described, the result would have been a well-organized kitchen. However, there are a number of other benefits that would have been achieved through this model (often referred to as "guided discovery learning"). First, you would have learned how to develop principles of fact investigation and research relevant to kitchen organizing and you would have developed the capacity to apply those principles in a specific factual context. Second, you would have learned how to identify choices that must be made (either by making a conscious choice or by failing to make a choice at all) and you would have developed the capacity to improve your decisionmaking process by reflecting on those choices as they were confronted. Third, you would have developed skills of kitchen organization from your ownership of this experience.

We capture all of these pedagogical goals (and many others) through the concept of the "reflective practitioner." What we hope to do through clinical methodology is to create a reflective practicum. In this setting, we will work together to help you develop into a practitioner who can identify the many moments in the lawyering process at which choices can be made ("choice moments"). And, we hope to help you develop into a practitioner who has a reason for every choice s/he makes and a process for making and implementing those choices that includes critical reflection through every step of your professional career.

B. Instructional Settings

We turn now to the specific settings we will use to try to achieve these pedagogical goals.

1. Live-Client Representation

It is difficult to over-emphasize the importance of the real-life aspects of clinical education. Justice Rosalie Wahl, a former chair of the ABA's Section of Legal Education and Admissions to the Bar and a member of the Minnesota Supreme Court, described the impact of live-client representation on student attorneys in the following terms: "I personally feel that the real consequences of working with a live client has a quality and an ethical responsibility to that person that you cannot experience by just listening about it." You will be given the opportunity to relate to people of backgrounds that will often be very different from your own. You will also find that you will have much to learn from your clients as you grapple with a model of representation in most legal clinics that maximizes client autonomy in decisionmaking.

Another benefit of real-life client clinical experiences relates to motivation. Many of you are familiar with the law school maxim—"First year they scare you; Second year they work you; Third year they bore you." Although you are likely to experience many feelings and emotions in clinic, boredom is not likely to be among them. You will be moving in clinic from the role of "spectator" to that of "actor." In doing so, the fact that you will have real people dependent on you will motivate you in powerful ways. Moreover, the fact that you will not want to be embarrassed before a judge, an adversary, or a supervising attorney necessarily means that you will approach your clinic responsibilities very differently from the ways that you approached class preparation in even the most demanding classroom settings.

Another significant benefit of live-client representation is the opportunity to identify and answer questions of professional responsibility that directly confront your role as a lawyer. Students are consistently amazed at how quickly ethical issues arise in their real-life cases and how the ethical rules come to life. You will also learn how difficult those issues often are to resolve in real-life practice.

2.   Making and Evaluating Choices

Clinic also uses two other methodologies that may be new to you. First, you will be asked to have a reason for every action you take. While that may seem like a fairly simple requirement, such reasons as "That's what the form book says" or "That's the way they do it at the firm where I work" are not going to cut it. Instead you will be asked to critically examine every opportunity at which a choice can and should be made and to develop thoughtful reasons for every decision you make. This approach will not guarantee that every decision is the "right" one—assuming that there even is a "right" one in many contexts. However, this approach will increase the *likelihood* that you will identify "choice moments" and make the right decisions with your clients by improving both your decisionmaking process and your process for implementing those decisions.

Second, you will be asked to address ambiguous situations throughout your clinical practice. These situations are ambiguous in two senses. You will not always have all the facts or legal authority that you might like to have. Reality places limitations on how much you can "know" and you will therefore have to frame and/or make decisions based on ambiguous information. These situations are also ambiguous in the sense that the outcomes of particular choices will not always be clear; they require you to grapple with "indeterminacy."

We will try to address both of these types of ambiguities by applying a risk-benefit matrix like the one below:

	High Risk	Moderate Risk	Low Risk
High Benefit	Possible— Very Hard	Probably— Fairly Hard	Yes— Easy
Moderate Benefit	Probably Not— Fairly Hard	Maybe— Very Hard	Probably— Fairly Easy
Low Benefit	No— Easy	Probably Not— Fairly Easy	Maybe— Pretty Easy

In this matrix it is fairly easy to identify and to avoid choices that have high potential risks and little potential benefits to your clients—choices in the lower-left box above. By using this matrix, you will also embrace choices that have high potential benefits and little potential risks to your clients—choices in the upper-right box above. The real difficulty is presented by choices in the upper-left box above—choices that have high potential benefits but also high potential risks for your clients—or moderate potential risks and moderate potential benefits—choices in the center box above.

This model depends on an ability to identify "choices" throughout our work. As we will discover, these "choices" are not always so obvious. Meeting a client in the law (clinic) office (an "automatic" for many people) should represent a decision that the office is the best place to meet in light of the various goals identified for that meeting. However, if this decision about location is not identified as a "choice moment," it will be impossible to assess the risks and benefits of different approaches to that "choice."

Once these choices are identified, we will work to look for ways to minimize those risks if possible while realizing those benefits. But, we will also discover that certain risks are unavoidable. These choices present among the most difficult decisions for lawyers and create an inherent anxiety that is part of the life of a practicing lawyer.

3. Case Supervision

Students need to regularly interact with their supervisors in a setting in which faculty members have sufficient time and energy to discuss case-related and personal issues with their students in an unhurried and non-directive manner. This generally requires a small student-to-faculty ratio—a significant departure from the large classes most of us have experienced as the norm throughout law school.

Although supervision styles vary from clinic to clinic and from supervisor to supervisor, there are some common features that you will experience in your clinic work. Students need to invest in the quality of their decisions—to own their clinic experiences. This process is facilitated by having supervisors help students reflect on their experiences and not by displacing students as the lawyers for their clients. The word "supervision" is therefore something of a misnomer. We will use it because most student practice rules use this term to describe the role of the clinical teacher. However, to the extent that it suggests a model in which your supervisor simply tells you what to do, we will use the term cautiously.

Supervisors will usually meet a student question with a question of their own to help you learn to discover not merely the answer to your question, but a process for finding answers to questions when supervisors are not available. This means that your question, "What do you think I should do here?" will often be met with the questions: "Well, what are your options? What do you see as the benefits and disadvantages of each option?" The goal here is *not* to "hide the ball" from you, but rather to help you discover the feel of the ball for yourself.

Despite the pedagogical reasons for this approach, times may arise in which your anxiety may exceed productive levels—periods in which your anxiety may begin to become debilitating. A little anxiety can be helpful as a motivating tool and some anxiety is inherent in the practice of law. However, too much anxiety can be destructive and can even become paralyzing. At those moments, be sure to share your feelings with your supervisor. Ordinarily, your supervising attorney will have picked up on these issues. However, in the event that you feel somewhat out of control, be sure to share this fact with him/her.

4.   Rounds

You are probably familiar, from doctor shows on television, with the technique of having interns and residents present client symptoms and treatment approaches to a physician and to other interns and residents, often at the patient's bedside. The goal of these "medical rounds" is to have others benefit from the experiences of the presenters to learn diagnostic tools and treatment approaches that may not be presented in their specific patient cases.

Although law clinic rounds take place out of the presence of clients, they serve a similar purpose. You will have the opportunity to learn from the experiences of other student attorneys in the clinic and to brainstorm and provide insights to others handling cases. You will also learn how to present your cases to others in a focused and accessible way—a skill that you will use in court and in dealing with adversaries.

5.   Seminar

Many clinic courses also offer a seminar to accompany your casework, a seminar that may not look too different from other seminar courses you have taken in law school. This seminar gives you the chance to learn some basic skills and values through a combination of lectures, discussions, and exercises before you begin and while you are providing real-life client representation. The seminar provides a vehicle for the transmission of the skills and values that you can apply in your real-life cases.

6.   Simulations

Many clinic courses also offer opportunities to engage in simulations. Simulations are exercises in which lawyering skills and values are developed and applied in a fictional factual context. These exercises are ordinarily based on real-life cases. However, because the exercises are artificial and because the interests of real-life clients are not at stake, you can be given wide latitude in the exercises and you can take risks and try techniques and styles of lawyering that you would not undertake with real-life client interests at stake.

Simulations are no substitute for live-client experiences. However, they offer benefits that make them a useful part of your clinical experience. Because simulated cases have controlled facts, simulations provide a uniformity of experience for all students in the class. Moreover, because real-life cases do not always develop in an orderly, controlled manner, simulations provide an opportunity for you to deal with discrete issues in a progressively more complex way. Videotape can also be used in simulations to allow you and your supervisor to critique your work in the simulated setting without disturbing the real-life lawyer-client relationship. Often these critiques are preceded by written self-evaluations.

Admittedly, simulations lack the factual complexity and uncertainty of real cases. Furthermore, it is hard to become emotionally involved or as motivated in simulation settings as in real-life. However, you will find that the more you can invest in the simulations and the learning opportunities they represent, the more you will gain from the opportunities presented.

C. Role of the Clients

Seminars, rounds, simulations, supervision. All of these methodologies are important parts of clinical education. However, no clinical methodology rivals in importance the role of clients and your work within the attorney-client relationship.

Professor Ann Shalleck described this phenomenon in her article, "Constructions of the Client in Legal Education."

> [T]he [clinical] model is based on a deeply contextualized understanding of who clients are and why they are significant. Students no longer see clients as abstract people with predetermined traits; rather, they see clients as unique individuals with particular characteristics situated within the real world.

Professor Shalleck went on to emphasize:

> [However,] [l]ive client clinics only present an opportunity, albeit a powerful one because of the immediacy and force of human relationships, to undermine the constructed client, as well as to develop and teach new methods for understanding and working with clients.

So, in clinic we will begin to undo the prevailing message of so much of law school—that cases are decided on "the law" and that clients can be reduced to a few "facts" excerpted in appellate decisions. Indeed, we will learn the critical importance of clients and their stories in the resolution of client problems. And, we will learn how to develop and present our client stories in the most effective ways to achieve our client goals.

D. Efficiency

Finally, as is probably evident to you from the various components that make up clinical methodology, clinic is a fairly expensive and labor-intensive form of legal education. However, these costs are incurred and these faculty resources are committed because there are many things that students can only learn in a clinical environment and other things that students can learn so much better in a clinical setting that the costs and resource allocations are easily justified.

Clinic is also a relatively inefficient way of providing legal services. When you enter the door to the clinic workspace for the first time, you might imagine the following sign hanging over the doorway:

Whereas efficiency is a necessary part of law practice, it is not a value within the clinical context.

If efficiency in representation were important, all of the representation would be provided by clinical supervisors—lawyers with experience in the areas in which the clients are seeking legal assistance. Instead, the focus in clinic is on ensuring professional competency while advancing educational objectives. This means giving you the space to find your own answers and, more important, your own questions.

E. Being Vulnerable

Many people get the message during law school that it is unwise to share weaknesses, that one must simply "tough it out." In any academic year, it is likely that the parent of a clinic student will get sick, that the romantic relationship of a clinic student will self-destruct, that the health of a clinic student may be impaired, that personal issues may intrude on the ability of a clinic student to fulfill his/her responsibilities. Whatever your feelings about being vulnerable generally, clinic is not a place to try to "tough it out."

Share information with your supervisor. While your supervisor will not be able to achieve miracles and certainly will not be able to make everything "right," s/he may be able to help you process the events intruding on your personal and professional lives. S/he may also be able to help take some of the pressure off you by arranging coverage for some of your work on behalf of clients or by addressing other needs. Without information about the need to compensate for these intervening events, it will be impossible for your supervisor to help you work through this.

F. Trying It Out

As one student wrote at the end of her clinical practice, "I experienced virtually every emotion possible in my work (happiness, sadness, frustration, anxiety, elation, sorrow, nervousness, apathy, elation . . . the list goes on)." That comment is fairly typical for the range of feelings that most students experience. Boredom is seldom a part of clinical education.

Your time in clinic will be relatively brief and you will want to learn as much as you possibly can about yourself and about the process of lawyering. To maximize the benefits, engage the various teaching methodologies throughout your clinical experience. At the same time, critically examine the various approaches to lawyering discussed. The more enthusiastically you invest in the clinical model and the less defensively you engage in the process of self-evaluation and self-criticism, the more you will gain from the experience. For most of you, this clinic course will be your only chance to "lawyer" with the support, oversight, and insights of a trained clinical supervisor. Make the most of this opportunity!

Chapter 3
Grading and Evaluation

Clinics vary widely from law school to law school and often from clinic to clinic within law schools in their approaches to grading and evaluation. Most clinics are now fully-graded credit courses. However, some law schools use a pass/fail or credit/no-credit system. Despite these differences, there are many fundamental characteristics that all clinical programs share.

All clinics evaluate student performance on three different models—an *absolute* model, a *relative* model, and an *individualized* model. In an *absolute* model, your performance as a student attorney will be compared to how a second- or third-year law student would be expected to perform. Your performance will be evaluated against a performance yardstick that varies little from semester to semester or year to year.

In the second model, the *relative* model, your performance will be compared to the performance of other students in the clinic during that semester or academic year. How you perform in your work in clinic will be compared to the work of the rest of the students and you will be evaluated (and ultimately graded) in comparison to your fellow students. This is similar to being graded on a curve.

In the third model, the *individualized* model, your work will be evaluated during your clinical experience based on how *you* performed compared to how *you* could have performed. It is individualized in the sense that it looks at *you*, as an individual, and looks at the strengths and weaknesses you brought to the clinic when you started and compares them to the strengths and weaknesses you possess when you leave the clinic at the end of the course. In this model, a student who grows significantly during the course of the clinic may be more highly evaluated than a student who starts out fairly strong, ends up fairly strong, but grows little in the process.

A. Process, Not Outcomes

Missing in all three of these models is an evaluation based on whether you "won" or "lost" your cases. There are several reasons for this, but there is one fundamental reason why outcome is not a criterion for evaluation. As you may already have discovered by observing lawyers in action, bad lawyers sometimes win cases despite their worst efforts and good lawyers sometimes lose cases despite their best efforts. Outcome is therefore a misleading guide in evaluating performance. Instead of looking at whether you won or lost, we will be looking at the process you used to assist your clients.

B. Evaluative Criteria

While clinics vary in the weight to be given to each of the three models of evaluation—absolute, relative, and individualized—clinics do share a wide range of criteria in evaluating performance under any of these models. These criteria look at performance in such areas as:

1. Relationships with Clients

Did you foster an effective attorney-client relationship with your clients? Did you respond in an empathic manner to your clients? Did you foster confidence in your clients? Did you advise your clients of significant developments in the case and of such major work products as briefs in support of motions? Did you advise your clients of significant dates, delays, and changes in schedules? Did you assist your clients in making all significant decisions in their cases by providing needed information and by helping the clients to structure the decisionmaking process? Did you educate your clients so that they will be better able to protect their own interests in the future?

2. Theory of the Client: Development and Implementation

How creative were you in developing theories of the client to accomplish your clients' goals? Did you conduct sufficient legal research to identify all possible theories? Did you develop sufficient facts to identify all appropriate theories? Did you identify factual inconsistencies in order to discard inappropriate theories? Did you utilize the full range of legal authorities available? Did you acquire sufficient substantive knowledge to develop all appropriate legal theories? How effectively did you implement the client theories? Did you develop sufficient facts to establish emotionally sensitive theories? Did you develop sufficient legal precedents to establish legally persuasive theories? Did you anticipate legal and factual arguments from adversaries and others? Was your legal research comprehensive and reliable? Did you identify all applicable rules of procedure? Were you able to use procedural and evidentiary rules to your clients' advantage?

3.   Practice Management

Did you coordinate your efforts with others? Did you consistently follow office procedures or have a reasoned and approved departure from those procedures? Did you meticulously maintain case files and document case activities? Did you commit the time required for course credits? Did you maintain a level of productivity that conformed to applicable standards? Did you meet all deadlines? Did you leave casework until the last minute? Did you allocate all of the time, effort, and other resources necessary to meet obligations to clients?

4.   Oral and Written Advocacy

Did you express your thoughts with precision, clarity, and economy? Did you express your thoughts in an organized manner? Did you express your thoughts in a format targeted to your intended audience (whether clients, adversaries or others)? Did you identify and use appropriate non-verbal aspects of oral communication? Did you identify and respond to verbal and non-verbal cues from others? Did your oral advocacy advance immediate and long-term objectives? Did you use proper grammar, vocabulary, pronunciations, and sentence structure? Did you articulate and enunciate clearly? Did you identify and use appropriate non-verbal aspects of written communication? Did you respond effectively to the positions expressed by others? Did your written advocacy advance immediate and long-term objectives?

5.   Professional Relationships

Did you interact effectively with adversaries? Did you interact effectively with court personnel? Did you interact effectively with witnesses? Did you respond courteously and with due consideration? Did you respond from positions of strength rather than from positions of weakness? Did you interact in a considerate and respectful manner with office staff? Did you interact effectively with your partner (if any)? Did you simply divide all tasks or did real collaboration take place in your work?

6.   Professional Responsibilities

Did you identify and address all possible conflicts with the Code of Professional Responsibility? Did you identify and address possible conflicts with other ethical, ideological, or personal considerations bearing on a case or the attorney-client relationship? Did you consult with the clinical supervisor appropriately? Did you advise the clinical supervisor of sensitive and significant matters? Did you advise the clinical supervisor of delays and changes in dates and schedules?

7.   Reflective Skills Development

Can you effectively criticize your own performance? Are you able to identify your strengths and weaknesses in the various areas of legal work? Did you gain insights about your future role as an attorney? Did you identify the aspects of lawyering that are important to you and the parts that are distasteful to you? Did you learn about the kinds of legal work that you want to do? Did you learn about the way that the legal system enforces norms? Did you learn about the value and limitations of lawyers in our legal system? Did you learn about the political and social contexts in which effective individual case analysis must take place? Did you gain insights about your future identity as an attorney?

8.   Participation in Class

Did you regularly attend class? Did you regularly read the assignments for class? Did you analyze the issues raised in the readings prior to class? Did you participate regularly in class discussions? Were you prepared to discuss developments in your cases in an effective manner with other students during grand rounds?

9.   Participation in Simulations

Did you participate effectively in simulations? Did you prepare in advance of the simulations? Did you effectively assume the role assigned? Were you prepared to address unexpected developments? Did you relate effectively to your "client" in the interviewing and counseling simulations? Did you relate effectively to opposing counsel in the negotiation simulation? Did you conduct a meaningful analysis of your performance and of your strengths and weaknesses in each self-evaluation? Did you participate in the videotaped critiques in an open and non-defensive manner? Did your performance as an attorney improve from your participation in the simulations?

10. Personal Development

Did you grow as a lawyer during the course of the clinic? Compared to your performance in the various aspects of lawyering at the beginning of the year, did you grow as an advocate during this year? Did you learn as much as you could have about yourself as an attorney? Did you do all you could have done to maximize the benefits you obtained from the clinical experience?

11. Miscellaneous

Many clinical programs also use a miscellaneous criterion to identify any aspects of your work in clinic that are not otherwise described in the preceding criteria. This miscellaneous criterion is designed to acknowledge work in fieldwork or seminar that deserves special recognition.

C. Earning Grades

What does this ultimately mean for grading and evaluation? Students tend to do well in their clinical work for several reasons. First, the intimacy of the relationships in clinic (especially the relationship between clinical supervisor and student) is such that students tend to work harder and do better than in their other classes. It is not possible to get "lost" in clinic in the way that a student can lose him/herself in a large class.

Second, for the first time in your life, you will have clients dependent on you and the work you do on their behalf. Students do not want to let their clients down and therefore perform better than in their other classes when choices affect only themselves. Students often surprise themselves by the ways that they translate these professional responsibilities into work on behalf of clients.

Third, students do not want to be embarrassed before judges, hearing officers, and adversaries. They therefore work harder than they might in a classroom course where the stakes are smaller. They know that they are giving away lawyering experience and (sometimes) substantive knowledge to opponents. Students therefore compensate in their preparation, in their dedication, and in their performance.

Finally, for the first time, students are personally subject to the Rules of Professional Responsibility in one or more jurisdictions. Meeting responsibilities under these rules for competent and ethical representation is usually a powerful spur for student performance. Students internalize these professional duties as they zealously advocate on behalf of their clients.

D. Continuous Feedback

Another difference between evaluation in clinic and in other classes is that evaluation in clinic is continuing. Rather than waiting for an end-of-semester examination and grade, evaluation in clinic occurs on a daily and ongoing basis. Especially to the extent that evaluation is based on an *individualized* model, the day-to-day growth in a student must constantly be observed and shared between student and supervisor.

E. Self-Evaluation

Another important characteristic of evaluation in clinic is the role of self-evaluation. Since one of the goals of clinical education is to develop in students the ability to continue to grow as a lawyer in practice, the ability to assess and criticize one's performance is a critical skill to be cultivated. This may be accomplished through formal self-evaluation exercises, through journals, or through oral interactions between student and supervisor. However, whatever the form of this self-evaluation, the goal is still the same.

You were admitted to law school and have succeeded in law school because of your achievements as a student. You are hard on yourself and use that self-criticism to push yourself forward. You may even take pride in declaring that you are "your own *worst* critic." Through clinic, the goal is to have you become "your own *best* critic"—to have you develop the ability to identify your strengths and weaknesses and to build on those strengths while minimizing those weaknesses.

So, the most significant mistake that you can make in clinic is not to learn from your mistakes. Mistakes may occur through inadequate decision-making or through inadequate implementation of those decisions. But, the identification of those mistakes and the sharing and processing of those mistakes with clinical supervisors and others will ordinarily represent a developing strength and one that will be rewarded through the evaluation process.

Chapter 4
Ethical Issues in Client Representation

One of the tangible effects of practicing as a student attorney in a live-client clinic is that you are now subject for the first time to the Rules of Professional Conduct of the jurisdiction or jurisdictions in which you will be practicing. Those responsibilities can be daunting. With that in mind, there are two cautions that should be stated at the outset:

1. THERE IS NO SUBSTITUTE FOR CAREFUL READING AND REREADING OF THE RULES OF PROFESSIONAL CONDUCT AND THE COMMENTS THERETO.

2. THERE IS NO SUBSTITUTE FOR CAREFUL READING AND REREADING OF THE RULES OF PROFESSIONAL CONDUCT AND THE COMMENTS THERETO.

With those two cautions in mind, we will focus on a few of the very common ethical issues that tend to arise early in practice. Students are constantly amazed at how quickly ethical issues come to life in the course of their clinical experience. As one student attorney exclaimed, "It is amazing to me how pervasive ethical issues are in practice."

These are by no means the only ethical issues you will confront. However, these are among the issues that most frequently arise early in the clinical context. They are also among the issues from which errors may be most difficult to recover.

Since rules of professional conduct vary somewhat from jurisdiction to jurisdiction, we will utilize the current ABA Model Rules of Professional Conduct (2000-2001) in addressing the ethical issues in the scenarios that follow.

Practice Scenario 1

You have been having trouble reaching a client by phone. However, the client does have an answering machine. Can you leave a message on the machine? If so, what can you say?

We start by referring to the applicable rules of professional conduct.

Rule 1.4 governs communications between lawyer and client. Subsection (a) of this rule provides that:

(a)   A lawyer shall keep a client reasonably informed about the status of a matter and promptly comply with reasonable requests for information.

Communication between lawyer and client is therefore strongly encouraged under the rule.

Rule 1.6 governs confidentiality of information. The rule provides that:

(a)   A lawyer shall not reveal information relating to representation of a client unless the client consents after consultation . . . .

Confidentiality is an important value under the rule. This requirement continues even after the death of the client.

Rules 1.4 and 1.6 create a tension for a lawyer. The lawyer wants to maximize communication with the client while protecting client confidentiality. However, maximizing client communication may create the risk of jeopardizing client confidentiality.

What messages would have the potential for raising concerns under the interface between these two rules? If the client is seeking assistance with a domestic violence situation and is still living with the victimizer, the mere fact that an individual unknown to the partner leaves a message might be sufficient to trigger an interrogation and reaction detrimental to the client. So, even a message as simple as, "Ms. Jones, please call Jane/John Smith" might be too much. By contrast, leaving a lengthy message on a home answering machine for a single parent living alone with small children may not present any problems.

Like many issues in clinic, we will have to tailor our response to the individual client and his/her unique situation. Any message presents some risk of disclosure of a secret or confidence. The question is what disclosure is reasonable under the circumstances in light of the need to advance the goals of the representation and the presence or absence of reasonable alternatives. If you leave a message that simply asks the client to call a particular telephone number, there is ordinarily minimal risk from disclosure, but also minimal likelihood of compliance. The more information you leave, the greater the risks from unintended disclosure and the greater the likelihood that the client will return your call. Like so much of what you will encounter in clinic, the answers are multi-textured and complex.

Practice Scenario 2

You received an important telephone call in one of your cases while your clinic partner was in class. You call your partner at home to share the information and get his/her answering machine. Can you leave a message about the content of the call?

This issue implicates the same rules of professional conduct and some of the same considerations as the prior problem. Does your partner live alone or in a group setting? Who will have access to the answering machine? Are there individualized mailboxes in the answering machine with some level of passcode security? How urgent is the communication and what alternatives are available for furthering the needed communication? Ultimately, is the communication reasonable under the circumstances?

Practice Scenario 3

A parent/friend/relative of your client brings your client to the office for the initial interview. The client asks this individual to stay with him/her throughout the interview process. Should you be concerned?

The answer is "Yes, you should be concerned." This problem is likely to arise in the course of your representation. And, it presents difficult tactical choices—choices not directly addressed by the Rules of Professional Conduct.

We start again with Rule 1.6 (discussed in the first practice scenario). However, the critical guidance is found in Comment 5 to the ABA Model Rules (2001 Edition). Comment 5 provides as follows:

> The principle of confidentiality is given effect in two related bodies of law, the attorney-client privilege (which includes the work product doctrine) in the law of evidence and the rule of confidentiality established in professional ethics. The attorney-client privilege applies in judicial and other proceedings in which a lawyer may be called as a witness or otherwise required to produce evidence concerning a client. The rule of client-lawyer confidentiality applies in situations other than those where evidence is sought from the lawyer through compulsion of law. The confidentiality rule applies not merely to matters communicated in confidence by the client but also to all information relating to the representation, whatever its source. A lawyer may not disclose such information except as authorized or required by the Rules of Professional Conduct or other law.

The attorney-client privilege prevents disclosure of most lawyer-client communications, except when those communications have been "published" to third parties. In this Practice Scenario, there are third parties (parties other than the lawyer and client) to whom the information is being published. Confidentiality as to the communications between lawyer and client may therefore be compromised by the presence of this third party.

Does that mean that the lawyer has the duty or the right to exclude the third party? Within the client-centered model of representation that we will be utilizing, the lawyer does not have either the right or the duty to exclude the third party from the interview. However, the lawyer does have the responsibility to bring this issue to the client's attention (preferably in a private moment), counseling the client about the risks and benefits of having a third party present, and then respecting the choices made by the client.

The presence of third parties in client meetings is further complicated when we consider the identities of the non-clients who are often brought into interviews by clients. What happens when the non-client is helping the client interpret from the language of the attorney to the language of the client? Does the fact that the non-client is not a certified interpreter affect the answer? What happens when the non-client is also providing information to the attorney during the interview about such issues as the political environment in the client's home country?

What happens when the non-client is a child of the client? Does the age of the child affect the issue of confidentiality? Should we reach a different decision if the child is a toddler than if the child is a teenager? What happens when the child is also helping communicate between lawyer and client? And, what happens when there are cultural issues that affect the interview process? For example, what happens if the attorney is a man and the client is a woman from a culture that prohibits her from being alone in a room with a man?

As you can see, the possible permutations and combinations that can arise in meetings with clients are almost infinite in variety. And, the extent to which a particular state bar ethics committee has addressed these issues varies greatly from state to state. It is therefore not possible to provide specific and definitive guidance here. The most that can realistically be done is to alert you to the complexity of this issue so that you can begin to address it in advance of your actual client interviews.

Practice Scenario 4

You and your partner are both fairly computer literate. Can you use e-mail to send messages and drafts of documents to your partner?

As e-mail communications have become more and more common in practice, more and more ethics committees have addressed this question. And, as e-mail communication has become more and more widely used, state bars have become increasingly accepting of e-mail as an ethical means of communication.

However, those jurisdictions that have considered the impact of e-mail on lawyer-lawyer and on lawyer-client communications have generally utilized a standard of reasonableness. These jurisdictions have recognized that no form of communication is completely immune from unwanted disclosure. So, e-mail communications are permitted in most cases if there is a reasonable expectation of privacy in their transmission and receipt. However, the rules also recognize that there may be certain situations in which the risks of unwanted disclosure are great and the benefits of instantaneous communication are small. In these cases, other, more secure, forms of communications should be utilized. And, if e-mail communication is utilized, encryption may be required to increase the protection of communications from unwanted disclosure.

It is also important to recognize that e-mail can take many different forms depending on the locations (in cyberspace) of the sender and recipient computers. E-mail communications can be sent through an internal office network, over land-based telephone lines directly connected to another computer, through a commercial network, or over the internet. An e-mail communication sent over the internet travels from the sender's computer through a host of intermediate computers owned by third parties to the recipient's mailbox. The message is broken up into different packets of information while traveling through third-party computers and is not reassembled until it reaches the recipient's computer. As we move from internal office network to internet, the potential for security breach increases and the need to protect against risks of interception or unwanted disclosure also increases.

The American Bar Association decided in Formal Opinion 99-413 that an attorney may transmit confidential information to clients or other attorneys using unencrypted e-mails sent over the Internet without violating the confidentiality requirements of Model Rule 1.6. The ABA based its decision on its determination that e-mail communication is no easier to intercept than other forms of communication that are considered to have a reasonable expectation of privacy. In further support, the ABA noted that e-mail communication is protected by the Electronic Communications Privacy Act of 1986 (which "provides criminal and civil penalties for the unauthorized interception or disclosure of any wire, oral, or electronic communication"). However, despite the ABA's conclusion that unencrypted e-mail is an acceptable form of communication which carries a reasonable expectation of privacy, the ABA also noted that attorneys must still consider the sensitivity of the material being transmitted and the consequences of interception. If materials are considered to be highly sensitive, the lawyer should consult with his/her client to consider if another more secure means of transmission should be utilized.

The majority of state ethics committees that have issued opinions on the appropriateness of electronic communications have decided, in accordance with the American Bar Association, that unencrypted e-mail communication with clients and other attorneys provides a reasonable expectation of privacy and, therefore, does not violate confidentiality requirements provided by the various state rules of professional conduct. While there is a consensus that e-mail communication provides a reasonable expectation of privacy, states differ on the amount of consent an attorney is required to receive from clients and the extent of precautionary measures that need to be taken in order to maintain this expectation of privacy for client communications. Moreover, at least one local bar, the Orange County Bar Association in California, has issued a formal opinion concluding that encryption is encouraged but not required and noting that "the wide availability of commercially unbreakable encryption software at affordable prices dictates that the prudent practitioner will investigate and use this technology."

Practice Scenario 5

Your client works part-time and finds it easiest to communicate with you at work. Can you send drafts of documents to her via fax? Can you communicate with her via e-mail?

There is little authority specifically addressing whether the use of fax machines to communicate with clients and other attorneys comports with confidentiality requirements. The lack of guidance may be due to the apparent assumption by courts that communication via fax meets the confidentiality requirements of Model Rule 1.6 and that such communication carries a reasonable expectation of privacy. (ABA Formal Op. 99-413, fn. 20) This assumption by the courts is most likely due to the fact that fax communications utilize the same means of transmission as landline telephone conversations, a method already determined to be sufficiently secure.

The main concern facing attorneys using fax machines to communicate with clients and other attorneys is the inadvertent disclosure of information contained in a fax once the transmission is completed. Fax machines are often located in the common area of an office and the information, once delivered, may be easily accessible to others.

There are obvious circumstances in which transmission of documents by fax should be avoided. For example, a client in a sexual harassment case might be still working for the same employer. In such a case, it would ordinarily be inappropriate to transmit information to the client by fax. Even if the employer does not intercept the document, the receiving fax machine may transmit journal entries that could provide the employer with relevant information about the potential challenge to its practices.

Attorneys must also be very careful when utilizing fax machines to avoid inadvertent disclosure of information to opposing parties or their counsel. Many jurisdictions have held that information, inadvertently sent to opposing counsel or party, is no longer protected or privileged. This is true even though American Bar Association Formal Opinion 92-368 provides that "[a] lawyer who receives materials that on their face appear to be subject to the attorney-client privilege or otherwise confidential, under circumstances where it is clear they were not intended for the receiving lawyer, should refrain from examining the materials, notify the sending lawyer and abide the instructions of the lawyer who sent them."

It is generally accepted that a lawyer has a reasonable expectation of privacy in communication with clients by mail and by land-based telephones. (ABA Formal Opinion 99-413) However, there are divided opinions on whether or not the use of cordless phones and cellular phones carry a similar expectation of privacy. Some authorities recognize privacy expectations for communications through these mediums; others find not enough security to protect the confidentiality requirements of Model Rule 1.6 or the expectation of privacy required for attorney-client privilege to exist.

Practice Scenario 6

You represent a wife in a custody matter. The husband calls and is accepted for representation by another clinic at the law school. Can the clinics represent both parties in different matters?

Your answer to this question depends on the application of Rule 1.7 to the Practice Scenario. Rule 1.7 governs "conflicts of interest." Subsection (a) of this rule provides as follows:

(a)   A lawyer shall not represent a client if the representation of that client will be directly adverse to another client, unless:

    (1)   the lawyer reasonably believes the representation will not be adversely affected; and

    (2)   each client consents after consultation.

Why is there a potential conflict of interest in the representation of a husband and wife when they are seeking assistance with totally different matters? Start by thinking about the information that will flow in the process of representing the husband in a tax matter. Information about the husband's financial situation, his sources of income and his assets, will be necessary to properly represent the husband. However, that same information would be very helpful to the lawyers representing the wife in seeking custody (and possibly support). That kind of conflict is exactly the kind of situation envisioned by Rule 1.7.

Different clinical programs address this potential conflict in very different ways. In many law schools, there is one entity—the clinical program. As in a single law firm, no clinic (or lawyer) can ethically do what cannot be done ethically in another clinic (or by another lawyer). By contrast, in other law schools, each clinic is a separate entity, like separate law firms, that happen to be located in the same building, much as different law firms might be located in the same office building.

There are important pedagogical and other reasons why law schools choose one model or another. However, whatever the reasons for the choice as to clinical program design, that choice has important implications for the determination of conflicts of interest.

Practice Scenario 7

During the summer, you worked at a major law firm. The clinic is now being asked to represent a client who is being sued by a party represented by that firm. Can the clinic accept this client? Does it make any difference if you did not work on this case?

This is another issue that will yield different answers depending on the jurisdiction(s) in which you practice. In some jurisdictions, an entire clinical program may be disqualified from representing the client because of a conflict of interest created by a single student. This situation is referred to as "imputed" disqualification. In other jurisdictions, students in the clinical program may be able to represent the client so long as the student presenting the conflict of interest is "walled off" from the representation. In some jurisdictions, if the student did not work on the "case," the student may still be able to participate in the representation.

These different approaches reflect different ways of balancing the ethical rules with the current realities of student work and intern/externship experiences. Many students now work in a variety of legal settings before and during the time that they are in law school. In order to encourage these experiences, some jurisdictions do not disqualify subsequent law firms and clinics based on the prior experiences of students. However, even in these relaxed "imputed disqualification" jurisdictions, these students may still be disqualified from knowledge of and participation in these matters.

By contrast, many jurisdictions do not recognize or encourage multiple law student experiences within their ethical rules. In these jurisdictions, each subsequent law firm or clinic could be disqualified based on the prior work experiences of a law student or lawyer. "Imputed" disqualification in these jurisdictions can have the effect of either limiting work experiences or greatly complicating the determination of conflicts of interest within clinical programs. You will therefore need to review your work experiences and the possible conflicts of interest that they may present with your clinical teachers.

Practice Scenario 8

Your case involves an allegedly defective vehicle sold by a car dealer to your client. Can you call up the mechanic who worked on the car for information about the servicing? What about the manager of the service department at the dealership? What about the general manager of the dealership?

This issue frequently arises in clinical and other settings. You need to get information to identify, evaluate and pursue a client's claims or defenses. That information is in the hands of others. What can and can't you do to get that information? The answer is found in the application of Rule 4.2 of the Rules of Professional Conduct.

Rule 4.2 governs "Communication With Person Represented by Counsel." It provides that:

> In representing a client, a lawyer shall not communicate about the subject of the representation with a person the lawyer knows to be represented by another lawyer in the matter, unless the lawyer has the consent of the other lawyer or is authorized by law to do so."

Comment 4 to this Rule provides that:

> In the case of an organization, this Rule prohibits communications by a lawyer for another person or entity concerning the matter in representation with persons having a managerial responsibility on behalf of the organization, and with any other person whose act or omission in connection with that matter may be imputed to the organization for purposes of civil or criminal liability or whose statement may constitute an admission on the part

of the organization. If an agent or employee of the organization is represented in the matter by his or her own counsel, the consent by that counsel to a communication will be sufficient for purposes of this Rule. . . . .

So, the question of whether and to whom we can communicate will depend on the scope of our representation—the goals for which legal assistance has been sought—and the power/authority of the employees of the party organization to help us achieve those goals.

The dealership may have a lawyer on retainer to assist it with consumer complaints and other issues. If it does not, then we are dealing with an unrepresented person and we will be subject to the limitations imposed by Rule 4.3 (discussed in Practice Scenario 10). If the dealership does have a lawyer, the mechanic might appear to be a safe party with whom to talk. However, in a case involving improper servicing of a vehicle, her/his acts or omissions could be imputed to the dealership and we therefore could not approach her/him without permission. The service manager also could not be approached. And, the manager of the dealership could not be approached without permission of opposing counsel. However, even within these parameters suggested by the model rules, different jurisdictions may impose more or less restrictive standards on communication by opposing lawyers.

Practice Scenario 9

You are representing a client who was cut off from welfare benefits. Can you contact the social worker at the welfare agency who took the action? Can you contact the worker's supervisor? What about the Director of the agency?

This Practice Scenario seems to raise the same ethical issues as Practice Scenario 8. However, the answer to this issue varies significantly because of the governmental status of the opposing party here and the application of the last clause of Rule 4.2, "or is authorized by law to do so." Comment 1 to Rule 4.2 explains this clause in the following terms:

Communications authorized by law include, for example, the right of a party to a controversy with a government agency to speak with government officials about the matter.

Why have the ethical rules carved out a special authorization to communicate more broadly with a governmental party than with a private party? The answer is found in the First Amendment's protection of the right to petition for redress of grievances. Since that amendment imposes a limitation on the power of government, ethical rules cannot take away the power to communicate with government officials—the essence of petitioning for redress.

Remember, however, that the fact that you may have the right to contact an opposing party does not mean that that party must communicate with you. Government lawyers frequently advise their clients not to communicate with outside lawyers outside their presence or without their permission. And, many individuals simply will not want to speak to you. We will talk more about this problem in the chapter on "Fact Investigation."

Practice Scenario 10

You are representing the wife in a divorce/custody case. You receive a call from the husband. Can you talk to him? If you can, are there any limitations on what you can say?

Because legal assistance, especially civil legal assistance, has become more and more limited over the past 30 years, lawyers frequently must interact with opposing parties who are unrepresented. *Pro se* parties present special difficulties for opposing counsel and also for judges and other court personnel.

Unsophisticated individuals must make their way through a complex and often foreign legal system. Judges may want to see justice done but must resist the inclination to try the case for the *pro se* litigant. Lawyers for opposing parties are placed in an especially difficult position. They don't want to take advantage of the lack of knowledge of the opposing party but they are also appreciative of the fact that that lack of knowledge makes it easier for them to achieve the goals of their clients.

To the extent that the rules of professional conduct are helpful in this arena, the relevant rule is Rule 4.3. Rule 4.3 addresses the issue of "Dealing With Unrepresented Person." It provides as follows:

> In dealing on behalf of a client with a person who is not represented by counsel, a lawyer shall not state or imply that the lawyer is disinterested. When the lawyer knows or reasonably should know that the unrepresented person misunderstands the lawyer's role in the matter, the lawyer shall make reasonable efforts to correct the misunderstanding.

So, under the rule we are told (at least theoretically) to advise the other party of our role in furthering interests potentially in conflict with his/hers and to advise him/her to seek independent counsel. In reality, the conversation more often sounds like this:

Lawyer: "I represent your wife and her interests are potentially in conflict with your interests. You should seek a lawyer to represent your interests."

Party: "I've tried to get a lawyer and no one could help me. What do you think that I should do?"

Lawyer: "I can't advise you since I represent your wife."

Party: "I understand that, but I don't understand what's going on here. What do you think I should do?"

The rule makes this problem seem an easy one for ethical lawyers. The reality is far more complex, especially for humane individuals who don't want to abuse their knowledge and status and their associated power within the legal system.

Practice Scenario 11

You are representing a debtor in a bankruptcy proceeding. You receive a call from the law firm representing one of the creditors. Can you describe yourself as counsel for the debtor?

The applicable rule of professional conduct is Rule 5.5. Rule 5.5 addresses the "Unauthorized Practice of Law." It provides as follows:

A lawyer shall not:

(a)   practice law in a jurisdiction where doing so violates the regulation of the legal profession in that jurisdiction; or

(b)   assist a person who is not a member of the bar in the performance of activity that constitutes the unauthorized practice of law.

The application of Rule 5.5 to the facts of the problem depends on the student practice rule in your jurisdiction, your status under that rule, and the design of the clinic in which you are working. Most student practice rules grant students who qualify under those rules a limited license to practice law in that jurisdiction. In effect, so long as the student fulfills the requirements of the applicable rule, including supervision by a qualified supervisor if required, that student operates as a lawyer.

However, that student should be extremely conscious of dotting every "i" and crossing every "t" in conducting that practice. Student practice rules ordinarily require students to identify themselves as *student* attorneys" or as "*certified* law students." And, those rules ordinarily require clinical supervisors to cosign pleadings.

There is another powerful reason for scrupulously observing the requirements of the applicable student practice rules. Much of the representation in clinics is conducted on behalf of clients who are otherwise disempowered in the legal system. Often, these clients have powerful adversaries represented by powerful attorneys. And, these adversaries and their lawyers are not afraid to raise the stakes for opposing client and lawyer in order to get their way.

Opposing counsel will often try to use every advantage that they can in achieving the goals of their clients. They may attempt to bully you or to intimidate you and they will often treat you in a condescending and patronizing manner. Exploiting a cheap advantage by raising a potential ethical claim against you is well within the repertoire of many such lawyers. It would therefore be a mistake to leave yourself and your client vulnerable based on alleged noncompliance with a student practice rule.

Chapter 5
Theory of the Client

Imagine that you are a contestant on the game show "Jeopardy." It is final Jeopardy, the subject is "Clinical Legal Education," and you are enmeshed in a close contest. In order to win you bet all of your earnings so far. Alex Trebek turns to the screen and the following clue appears: "The most important concept you will learn in clinic." You begin to write down your answer as Alex cautions, "Remember to phrase your answer in the form of a question." And your answer is . . . "What is theory of the client?"

There is no concept that will more directly affect your career as a lawyer than client theory. And, there is no lawyering concept that you will utilize more frequently in your work. It will affect every aspect of your legal work on behalf of clients. So, what is "theory of the client?" And, if it is so important, why haven't you heard about it in law school before?

A. Defining our Terms

"Theory of the client" is the sum of the legal and non-legal strategies that can be created to achieve the goals of the unique individual you represent. This range of approaches may include options that are complementary or that are mutually exclusive. The approaches may advance some or all of the client's goals. However, they are always goal-oriented; they are driven by the needs of the client and must have at least some potential to achieve one or more of the client's identified goals.

B. Scope of the Concept

Theory of the client includes non-legal (but not illegal) as well as legal strategies; lawyers are not limited to suggesting legal approaches to achieve client goals. Business lawyers often advise business clients about business decisions outside of contract formation or business litigation. Family lawyers often counsel family law clients about domestic decisions independent of filing for divorce or other family law interventions. Often a non-legal strategy will provide a more direct, less expensive, and faster strategy for achieving a client's goal(s). However, "theory of the client" will also ordinarily include legal strategies as well—strategies that often reflect the reasons why the client sought legal assistance in the first place (even if the actual approaches include options unimagined by the client when s/he sought assistance).

The critical focus here is on the words "of the client." We will be working with a client to devise an approach or a range of approaches to meet the unique needs of *that* client in light of *that* client's constellation of family, friends, experiences, goals, dreams, needs, problems, and other factors. Just as a sports car may be a very nice vehicle for a childless individual, a mini-van may be far preferable for an individual with children. Our goal is to work with a client to devise the unique set of approaches that will most likely achieve that client's goals and then to implement effectively those approaches.

C.   Theory of the Case

Frequently our client theories will include one or more approaches that involve litigation or other legal action. We will refer to these legal approaches by the term "theory of the client's case" or by the more streamlined term "case theory." In doing so, however, we will be careful to remember that our clients are not "cases." And, we will remember that different clients confronted with similar legal problems may have different goals, may present different facts, and may require different strategic approaches. Despite these potential shortcomings, we will use the term "case theory" because it allows us to tap into the growing body of legal knowledge regarding this concept.

We can think of case theory as an integration of the *facts* surrounding the client (the client's "story") and the *law* relevant to the client's concerns. The purpose of case theory is to tell a persuasive story—sometimes to a factfinder (judge or jury), but often to an adversary or other individual. Our goal is to persuade that audience to do something for our client—to decide a case in our client's favor, to accept a negotiated settlement favorable to our client, to forego litigation against our client. Case theory must therefore be designed to achieve the client's goals and can only be developed in reference to those goals.

D.   Role of Case Theory

As we will discover, case theory is all-pervasive. Case theory explains the facts, relationships, and circumstances of the client and other parties in the way(s) that can best achieve the client's goals. Case theory therefore represents the organizing principle for all of our representation activities on behalf of our client; it ties together and directs all of our work.

The role of case theory is not always so obvious for students (or lawyers). In one clinic jury trial, students were representing a young man charged with attempted daytime housebreaking (the statutory equivalent of attempted burglary during daylight hours). The client's "story" was that he was walking around the neighborhood looking for odd jobs (cleaning gutters, raking leaves) and that was why he was knocking on doors and looking in house windows for occupants. The prosecution "story" was that the client was "casing" the neighborhood, looking for vacant houses to break into. Both stories were described during the respective opening statements.

The jury had been impaneled during the morning and the direct examination of the first witness, a police officer, was completed before lunch. The direct examination seemed fairly uneventful. The police officer testified to having received a report of a suspicious person in the neighborhood knocking on doors and peering in windows. The police officer then testified that he had observed the defendant in the neighborhood and had arrested him in response to that report.

At the conclusion of the direct examination, the judge declared a recess for lunch. But, before breaking for our lunch, the students and I sat down together to talk through their plans after lunch. They were very excited about the direct examination and declared, "We are really going to be able to get that police officer after lunch!" I then asked them to tell me what their plans were for cross-examination. They pointed out that the officer had testified that he had received a report of a suspicious person wearing a black shirt and white pants, but that the report after the arrest stated that the defendant was wearing a navy blue shirt and light tan pants. This "discrepancy," they pointed out, would give them plenty of ammunition for impeachment.

I then asked them whether they were going to claim mistaken identity and that the police officer had arrested the "wrong" suspicious person. No, they explained, the case theory they intended to present hadn't changed. Then, I asked, "How would the minor discrepancy in color of shirt and pants further their case theory that the defendant was there for a different purpose from the one ascribed to him by the police?" The students looked at each other for a moment and you could almost see the light bulb above their heads illuminate. "So," they exclaimed, "That's why case theory is so important!"

And, yes, that *is* why case theory is so important. Case theory is the lens through which your client's life experiences are filtered and through which your legal research and analysis is assessed. It is the theme that provides a context for everything you do and that gives meaning to your fact investigation and legal research. And, it is in relation to your case theory that you evaluate whether evidence hurts or helps your case (theory) and whether an objection that could be made should be made (whether the question and likely answer will hurt your case theory).

E. The Dynamic Nature of Client Theory

However, client theory is not a static concept. A lawyer begins to develop possible client theories in (and sometimes before) the client interview. Client theories then evolve based on client decisionmaking, fact development, and legal research. The client may discard certain theories; fact investigation may demonstrate that certain theories cannot be proven; legal research may force you to conclude that certain theories cannot be supported under the law. By the time of trial (if a case proceeds that far), the various client theories have ordinarily been winnowed down to a single case theory that can be presented in a coherent way to the factfinder.

F. Deconstructing Case Theory

Let us therefore look at the use of case theory by first deconstructing it into its two components: factual theory and legal theory. In order to prevail, we will need to develop a factual theory that can be proven to the satisfaction of a factfinder or adversary. And, in order to prevail, we will need to develop a legal theory that can persuade the judge or opponent.

1. Factual Theory

The factual theory is the client's "story" accessorized by our fact investigation and presented through witnesses, exhibits, and other documentary evidence. It presents a view of the facts that will justify relief under some legal theory. Ideally, it should be based on all the information and logical inferences in the case—making sense of all the evidence that will be received.

2. Factual Theory Versus the "Facts"

Although a good factual theory needs to make sense of all of the evidence, factual theory and reality are not necessarily the same. While lawyers cannot knowingly present false testimony, it is often impossible to know exactly what happened in and around an event. In a divorce, the lawyer may hear from her client, the husband, and may depose the wife. As a result of that process, the lawyer may hear two completely contradictory stories of the substantively critical events. Both stories cannot be completely accurate, but both stories may be honestly told. And, the "truth," if it could be divined, might be contained in neither story or might be contained equally in both.

This concept is sometimes captured by the phrase "Rashomon." In the classic Japanese film by that name, based on two short stories by Ryûnosuke Akutagawa, the acclaimed director, Akira Kurosawa tells us the story of several people seeking shelter at the crumbling "Rashomon Gate" in Kyoto, Japan. To pass the time, some of the travelers tell a story about an incident in which a woman is raped and her husband is killed.

Each storyteller tells a story of the "same" events, but each story is profoundly different. Each story is honestly told, but the stories cannot all be true, even as one of the storytellers proclaims, "I don't tell lies" and delivers a second version of his story that contradicts his first. Which of the stories is "true?" Are any of the stories "true?" And, how would we, as the audience for the various stories, make that determination? As critic James Berardinelli has noted, the film reminds us of "the inability of any one man to know the truth, no matter how clearly he thinks he sees things. Perspective distorts reality and makes the absolute truth unknowable."

NON SEQUITOR © Wiley Miller. Dist. by UNIVERSAL PRESS SYNDICATE. Reprinted with permission. All rights reserved.

A factual theory is therefore not the facts. It is simply one version of what the facts might be. This Wiley cartoon accurately captures the dilemma faced by many factfinders. Neither party's factual theory may be historically accurate; yet, the jury must choose between them anyway.

3.   Focus of the Factual Theory

A good factual theory needs to withstand three types of attacks. First, your factual theory must be able to withstand attacks based on factual sufficiency (*i.e.*, sufficient credible evidence must be presented on each of the elements of a claim or defense to allow the judge or jury to find in your client's favor). This requirement means that you will need to examine each of your causes of action (or affirmative defenses), break each cause of action (or affirmative defense) down into its component elements, and identify the evidence you intend to present to demonstrate each of these elements. Elements of your claims or defenses may be derived from statutes, regulations, and case law. However, lawyers often use tools like pattern jury instructions to facilitate this process.

Second, your factual theory must be able to withstand attacks based on persuasive sufficiency (*i.e.*, the judge or jury has to be persuaded to find in your favor on each of the elements of a claim or defense on which you have the burden of proof). Third, the factual theory must be able to withstand independent attacks by the other side (*i.e.*, attacks based on such arguments as affirmative defenses).

4.   The Legal Theory

The legal theory is a legal framework developed from interpretation, analysis, and expansion of legal rules and standards (found in cases, statutes, regulations, law review articles and other sources). A good legal theory attempts to utilize the law as currently established (because it is a lot easier to persuade someone about what the law is when that interpretation is already reflected in "the books"). However, a lawyer must not be afraid to expand the law if the existing law is adverse to your client and his/her claims or defenses.

When civil rights lawyers began the effort to establish that de jure segregation in public schools was unconstitutional, the "law" was directly against them. *Plessy v. Ferguson* was the "law of the land" and that "law" said that "separate but equal" was constitutional. The lawyers in the cases culminating in *Brown v. Board of Education* could not prevail if *Plessy* remained good law. So, as described in the book SIMPLE JUSTICE, the lawyers embarked on a strategy to change the law by biting off small pieces of *Plessy* one at a time. These other cases would take place in contexts that would be less directly threatening to the public than desegregation in public education. However, by the time that de jure segregation in public education was before the court, much of *Plessy's* vitality would have been destroyed.

So, we will try to use the law as it exists, but we will not be afraid to argue for an expansion of the law if it is necessary for our client to prevail. And, as we develop theories for our clients, we will be conscious of the fact that law can be changed in legislatures, in courts, and in administrative agencies. Finally, we will remember that just as a factual theory is only one side's view of the facts, so a legal theory is not *the* law, but only one side's interpretation of the law.

G. Reunifying Case Theory

It is often helpful to think about the component parts of case theory. However, it is important to remember that although factual and legal theories are theoretically separate, they are so interrelated that it is usually better to think of them as simply two different components of the same "story." The legal theory gives context to the factual theory—it helps us understand why the facts are important. The factual theory makes the factfinder want to decide the law in our favor—to find a legal hook on which to hang the facts.

In representing a client seeking a civil protection order to protect her from domestic violence, two student attorneys were concerned that the client's story of the most recent incident might not be sufficiently powerful to persuade a judge to issue a protection order. However, they conducted legal research and discovered that the state's highest court had ruled that evidence of prior incidents could be introduced to persuade a judge of the seriousness of the most recent incident. They then went back to the client to further explore the history of her relationship with her husband. Ultimately they presented a story on behalf of the client that began in the past and ended with the most recent incident. And, after prevailing over objection on the relevance of the testimony of prior incidents, the student attorneys were able to persuade the judge that the client had a well-founded fear of physical violence as a result of the latest, more ambiguous, incident.

Of course, there is at least one type of case theory that does not attempt to argue either the facts as they are presented or the law as it currently exists (or as it might be changed). That type of case theory is "jury nullification." In jury nullification, political context takes the place of legal theory. In such a case the defense attorney may argue that the law enforcement system is so corrupt that the factfinder does not need to assess either the facts or the law. Instead, the defense argues, the factfinder should punish the law enforcement system for its historical pattern of abuses to particular populations by acquitting the defendant.

H. The Client as a Component of Case Theory

We will also be conscious of the impact of our client on factfinder acceptance of our case theory. Whether our client testifies or not, the client's "presence" will constantly be used as a measuring stick against which case theory will be compared. We will therefore work hard to ensure that our client's "presence" is consistent with the vision created by our case theory.

In a clinic case, two students represented a young black male charged with auto theft. The judge assigned to the case had a well-deserved reputation for racism and the students faced a significant task in even getting the judge to listen to the evidence. However, they were very conscious of the impact of client presence on case theory and worked diligently with the client over a period of weeks in preparing him for the trial. One of the things that they did was to videotape the client in mock hearings and to allow the client to critique his own performance—to allow him to reinvent himself as a criminal defendant in an unfair system.

Rather than simply tell the client what to wear and how to behave in the courtroom, the client was able to try out different approaches and to assess them for himself. He decided, for example, not to wear a suit to the trial (because he felt that it would make him look phony) but rather to wear nice school clothes. He learned to look the judge in the eye, to naturally stand when the judge entered or left the courtroom, and to present a demeanor inconsistent with the judge's expectations.

Several courtrooms summoned juries on the morning of the trial and the jury pool was inadequate to meet the needs in all of the courtrooms. Because our case was more current than several of the others, we had to wait while juries were empaneled in the other courtrooms first. We would then effectively get the rejects from the other courtrooms—not always a desirable outcome.

Over the course of the morning, the judge came in periodically to tell us that there was no jury panel yet and that he would come back in an hour or so to give us an update. On each occasion, the client stood up on his own, looked the judge respectfully in the eye, and thanked the judge for the information. When lunchtime came, the process was repeated again and we continued the same pattern several times in the afternoon.

Finally, as the day was coming to a close, the judge came out and said that while the case could be put over until tomorrow, he felt that he had gotten to know the defendant over the course of the day. He opined, rather patronizingly, that he did not know if our client had really committed the acts charged, but that he was convinced that even if he had, it was an aberration in his behavior and would not be repeated. He therefore asked the prosecuting attorney if she would accept probation before judgment if the client pleaded guilty to a lesser charge of unauthorized use of a vehicle. (In probation before judgment, a criminal defendant who successfully completes his probation never has a record of a criminal conviction.) The judge then explained to the defendant that if he pleaded guilty to the lesser charge, the judge would strike his guilty plea, put him on unsupervised probation, end his probation that day, and expunge his arrest. The prosecuting attorney grudgingly accepted the judge's proposal; the client entered his plea (after a discussion with the student attorneys); and the client's criminal exposure was terminated.

While that may seem like a bizarre outcome in a criminal "justice" system, it represents a reality of the system with which we all must contend. In fact, as represented in this cartoon, the opposite outcome often occurs as well. Being unappealing is often far worse than being guilty.

"Ask the judge whether we can find the defendant not guilty and still execute him."

I.   Levels of Case Theory

We should also be conscious of not falling into the trap of narrowly answering the question, "What is your case theory?" by saying "Negligence" or "Self-Defense." Instead we will think about developing case theory as a three-step process. We will tell a story about our client and his/her facts; we will link that story to the law as it exists or as we believe it should exist; and, we will reach a conclusion based on the facts and the law that has the potential for realizing our client's goals.

While we will not fall into the trap of creating one-word case theories, we will also be conscious of the benefits of capturing our case theories in phrases that are accessible to factfinders. Think for a moment about the case theory used by the defense in the O.J. Simpson criminal trial. Their case theory was that Nicole Brown Simpson had been killed by drug dealers and that O.J. Simpson had been set up by a racist police force that had planted blood samples on the scene to link O.J. Simpson to the crime. Whatever our views about that defense, the defense case theory played effectively to the experiences of the factfinders (the jury) and attempted to explain all of the evidence in a coherent and persuasive way.

At the same time, the defense case theory could be reduced to a single phrase that was visually effective and that resonated powerfully. Johnnie Cochran told the jury: "If it doesn't fit, you must acquit." Each time he used this phrase, it was a shorthand reminder of the entire defense case theory— symbolized by a pair of gloves that were allegedly too small and that, the defense argued, could only have been left at the scene to implicate O.J. Simpson by a dishonest and racist police force.

J.   Creating a Good Case Theory

We will also be conscious of the elements that make up a good theory of the case. A good case theory is:

Consistent with the client's wishes

The case theory should present a picture of the client and his/her story that is acceptable to the client. This sometimes presents difficult counseling issues. It may be possible to get a client released on a criminal charge or relieved of a contractual responsibility by presenting the client as a "pathetic" individual. However, the client may be unwilling to be presented in that light.

Consistent with the client's short and long-term goals

The case theory should, if possible, address all of the client's goals— short, medium, and long-term. However, that may not be possible in all situations. In such situations, the client may have to choose between short and long-term goals and/or among and between various short or long-term goals. Again, this will present difficult counseling problems in helping the client work through the task of choosing between inconsistent goals.

Consistent with the facts

The case theory should make use of strong evidence and explain away bad or inconsistent facts. Bad facts will not simply go away (as fervently as we may wish them to). Instead, we need to design a case theory that takes advantage of powerful witnesses and persuasive documentary evidence and that anticipates and defuses the pieces of our opponent's case theory that undercut our client's story.

Consistent with the law

The case theory should start with the law as it currently exists. However, as we have noted, we need to be willing to argue for expansion of the law if it is necessary for our client to prevail.

Persuasive

The case theory needs to persuade a factfinder. We will talk more about the factors that make a "story" persuasive in the chapter on "Fact Investigation." However, case theories must ultimately be accepted by an audience. Even the most elegant case theory will therefore fail if it does not persuade.

Credible

The case theory needs to be believed by the factfinder. As we will discuss in the section on "Fact Investigation," there are a number of factors that affect the credibility of the story that makes up the factual theory part of case theory. The story needs to do more than simply tell what happened at the "substantively critical moment." Factfinders generally like stories that have a beginning ("Once upon a time"), a middle ("And a dragon menaced the small village"), and an end ("And they all lived happily ever after"). Factfinders generally like stories that tell *why* things happened in a particular way, not merely *what* happened. These factors and more affect the credibility of case theories.

Appealing emotionally

The case theory should also appeal to the emotions of the factfinder. While we tend to think about persuasiveness in rational terms, often a case theory is successful because it appeals to the emotions of a factfinder and makes him/her/them want to decide in our favor. Even in a "small" case, we neglect the emotional content of our case theory at our own (and our client's) peril.

Comprehensive

The case theory should explain all of the circumstances of the case. It is human nature to want to have all of the facts, circumstances, and relationships of the parties tied up in a neat little package. While that may not always be possible, to the extent that we can make everything "fit" together, we increase the likelihood of achieving our client's goals.

K. Starting Wide, Ending Narrow

As we begin the process of working with our clients, we will cast a very wide net for possible client theories. Early on we will not know enough about how the facts or the law will develop to help the client make informed decisions about which case theories to pursue. Early on we will not have the relationship with the client to help him/her effectively sort through the benefits and disadvantages of specific client theories. Early on we will also not have enough information about our opponents and their counsel and the factfinders to know which theories are likely to resonate best with which audiences.

As the case develops, we will begin to narrow case theories with our client. We will narrow these case theories based on fact gathering, legal research, and client decisions. We will also make choices of which case theories to fully develop based on the funds available for fact investigation and legal research and based on other priorities. Finally, if we reach the point of trial, we will limit our case theories to one or two compatible case theories because factfinders usually do not respond well to inconsistent case theories—to a criminal defense that the client was not on the scene and if s/he was it was self-defense anyway.

Chapter 6
Client-Centered Representation

You probably have already noticed in your reading of the preceding chapters that clients loom large in our model of representation. We develop theories in reference to our clients and their unique facts and goals. We implement those theories to achieve client goals and with reference to the strengths and weaknesses in our clients' stories. And, we measure the effectiveness of our efforts in light of the extent to which we have furthered those client goals.

This emphasis on the role of the client is often referred to by the term "client-centered," a concept that was greatly advanced by the work of David Binder and Susan Price in their groundbreaking 1977 textbook, LEGAL INTERVIEWING AND COUNSELING: A CLIENT-CENTERED APPROACH. This concept was furthered and refined by the later work of Binder, Price, and Paul Bergman, by Robert Bastress and Joseph Harbaugh, and by such commentators as Stephen Ellmann and Robert Dinerstein. However, because the meaning of the term "client-centered" has changed over time and because different people mean different things when they use the term, we will define the phrase for our purposes here in both positive and negative ways.

A. Defining the Term Operationally

Client-centeredness affects two fundamental aspects of the lawyer-client relationship. First, it affects the focus of the legal representation; it places the client and the achievement of the client's goals at the center of everything that we do. While that focus may seem obvious, many lawyers practice with their own goals paramount. These attorney goals may include increased status, increased compensation, and increased fame. While we will acknowledge attorney needs, we will work hard to prevent them from intruding on our lawyer-client relationships.

Second, client-centeredness affects the process of the legal representation; it expands the role of the client as decisionmaker and colleague in the lawyer-client relationship and places additional demands on the lawyer to make this role a reality. For example, we will discover that it is insufficient to merely present options to a client for decisionmaking. Instead, we will work hard to make that decisionmaking process meaningful through our work in client counseling.

B. Giving Up Control

Lawyers do not always want to cede decisionmaking authority to their clients. After all, didn't we go to law school to develop the expertise that allows us to make better decisions than our clients would on their own? There are two responses to this question.

First, there are ethical restrictions on the role of the lawyer in the lawyer-client relationship. Under rule 1.2 of the Rules of Professional Conduct, the client must make decisions about the objectives or goals of the representation and the lawyer must consult with the client as to the means by which these objectives or goals are to be achieved. Although the distinction between goals and means is not always clear, in the client-centered model we will involve the client in decisions and at a level beyond the minimum envisioned by the ethical rules.

Second, although we developed expertise in law school, most of our expertise relates to analysis, not decisionmaking. Moreover, even to the extent that we believe that we are good decisionmakers, in relation to what value system would we be making decisions? Since client theories can only be evaluated with reference to the goals of a specific client based on that client's constellation of needs and dreams, we are hardly in the best position to make decisions that depend on information to which we may only have partial access.

Despite these reservations, we must recognize that as we develop relationships with our clients and become more invested in their lives, we also begin to become more and more invested in not wanting to see them make "bad" decisions. As we will discuss later in the chapter on counseling, yielding decisionmaking authority is often easier said than done. "The decision is yours to make," often means that, "The decision is yours to make so long as you agree with my recommendation."

Despite this recognition and despite (or perhaps because of) the fact that you are new to the profession, you may be susceptible to the inclination to want to push their clients in the "right" direction. Some of this tendency comes from the insecurity and anxiety we feel in our new role as "attorney," but some of it is the inevitable by-product of visions of lawyering presented to us in movie and television portrayals of lawyers. Few of these visions portray lawyers who operate in a client-centered way. Instead, we struggle with television and movie images lawyers who operate "effectively" within a lawyer-centered model for the "benefit" of their clients. However, that "benefit" is often evaluated by the lawyer in light of the lawyer's value system, not the client's.

C. Uniqueness of the Client

In addition to keeping the client at the center of the lawyer-client relationship, in the client-centered model the client is treated as a unique individual—different from the clients who came before and from those who will come after. This uniqueness means that unique solutions will be required to solve unique problems in light of the unique social, economic, cultural, and relational environment in which the client lives. One client seeking a divorce is not treated the same as any another client seeking a divorce; one client confronting an auto repossession is not treated the same as any another client in a similar situation; one client charged with battery is not treated the same as any other client charged with battery.

D. Holistic Lawyering

Another aspect of client-centeredness, closely related to our focus on uniqueness, is a focus on the "whole" client. We will be concerned with developing and implementing solutions that address the goals of the "whole" client. Like the models of "holistic" medical care, we will recognize the place of our legal assistance in the client's "big picture."

In criminal representation, consider, for example, an apparently good plea bargain that provides for a suspended sentence but substantial back-up time (time that the client would have to serve in prison if s/he violated her/his probation). Such a plea bargain cannot be effectively evaluated (and the client counseled about the wisdom of accepting the plea bargain) without evaluating the client's overall strengths and weaknesses and the likelihood that the client will actually be able to satisfy the requirements of supervised probation. Otherwise, it may be far more desirable for the client to serve a short sentence immediately and be free of state monitoring.

Or, in a consumer matter, we may have the opportunity for a negotiated settlement on behalf of our client. However, that settlement might be framed in many different ways—by, for example, providing for a lump-sum payment or a life annuity or through provision of in-kind services. How would we effectively counsel a client about the benefits or disadvantages of any form of settlement without knowing about the impact of any form of settlement on the client's receipt, for example, of governmental benefits?

E. Defining the Scope

Even within a holistic model, there are often limits. Clinics vary significantly from school to school and within schools. Some clinics are "subject matter" clinics. These include tax clinics and consumer law clinics, criminal defense clinics, and special education clinics. Representation in these clinics focuses on a single area of the law.

Other clinics are population-based. These include clinics that focus on women or on immigrants or on Native Americans. In population-based clinics it is far easier to address the needs of the whole client since the clinic does not purport to compartmentalize (or limit) representation to particular subject areas. However, even in these clinics students seldom provide representation through the full range of issues on which they might be able to provide assistance. So, we will be conscious of the benefits of "holistic" legal representation, of representing the "whole" client, while identifying the practical tradeoffs imposed by the real-life need to limit that representation in specified ways.

F. A Helper, Not a Mere Servant

Client-centered lawyers are often described as helpers, advisers, and counselors. However, being client-centered does not mean that you, as a lawyer, must or should automatically do everything that your client wants you to do. There are ethical limitations on what you can do on behalf of your clients—one of the most obvious is a prohibition on knowingly presenting false or perjured testimony. Moreover, a client is not necessarily well-served by pursuing client desires without critically analyzing and challenging those choices. And, sometimes, lawyers simply need to say, "You have the right to make the final decisions, but I do not have to be the lawyer to implement them."

Therefore, although the client-centered model can minimize attorney-client friction, client-centeredness is neither a panacea nor a guarantee of good client relationships. Sometimes, clients will simply not want to hear what you have to say and will shop for a lawyer who will give them the advice they seek. In such cases, the combination of client-centeredness and personal integrity will allow you to feel good about what you do as a lawyer, even if you may not always be able to tell your clients what they want to hear.

Ethical responsibilities also require lawyers to tell clients what they may not want to hear. In upholding an award of sanctions under Rule 11 against a plaintiff's attorney, a Circuit Judge cited the warning of famed trial attorney Elihu Root that, "About half of the practice of a decent lawyer is telling would-be clients that they are damned fools and should stop." This warning also harkens back to the vision of lawyer as "conscience" captured in the statement by Louis Brandeis that, "Half the time the practice of law consists of telling clients that they can't do what they want to." A client-centered model of representation may make a client more receptive to "bad" news and less hostile to the attorney delivering the news. However, as indicated in the following cartoon, it will neither eliminate the sting of bad news nor will it eliminate the risk of alienating the client.

G. Keeping Client Needs Paramount

While we will be conscious of the risks of lawyer-centered representation, we must also be conscious of the ways in which *our own* needs can interfere with the ways in which options are evaluated and presented to clients even in a client-centered model. Again, we will talk about this more in the chapter on counseling, but let us begin that process here.

As student attorneys we may be fearful about trying a case in court. Most probably, we have never done this before and the stakes for our client will be great. Can that anxiety cause us to more favorably evaluate options that avoid a trial (for example, by positively evaluating a proposed settlement)? Of course it can. Should our anxiety play a role in how we present options to our client? Of course it should not.

As student attorneys we may be looking forward to trying our first case in court—to show off our trial practice skills and to wear that dark blue suit that our parents bought us. Can that desire lead us to more favorably evaluate options that will give us the opportunity for a trial (for example, by negatively evaluating a proposed settlement)? Of course it can. Should our desire to try the case play a role in how we present options to our client? Of course it should not.

How will we achieve this model of a client-centered lawyer? The most honest answer is: "With great difficulty!" It is not easy to be client-centered in a world in which so many of our lawyer models do not embrace this role definition. It requires us to be aware of our own values and to avoid imposing those values on our clients. It requires us to be honest and genuine in our dealings with our clients. It requires us to communicate early and often with our clients and to communicate in ways that are actually accessible to our clients. It requires us to respect our clients and to demonstrate that respect in our dealings with our clients. And, it requires us to be empathic (or empathetic)—to work to understand what our clients are feeling and to "reflect" that understanding back to our clients.

The process goal of these four skills and values—genuineness, concreteness, respect, and empathy—is to facilitate communication between lawyer and client. By facilitating communication, we encourage an atmosphere of honesty and openness. We also make it more likely that "good" decisions will be made and that these decisions will be effectively implemented through a process in which lawyer and client are both fully invested. Again, however, the practical application of these skills and values is often much easier said than done.

H. Strengths and Weaknesses

A client-centered approach to representation works better at some lawyering stages than at others. It facilitates fact gathering and identification of options. It also increases the likelihood of thoughtful consideration and balancing of options. But, client-centered representation can sometimes result in a preoccupation with identification and evaluation of options at the expense of choosing between options and implementing those choices. Like some of the "talking therapies" in counseling, it is sometimes difficult to "fish or cut bait"—to make choices and to move forward with those choices.

I.   Justifying the Effort

If it requires so much effort to be client-centered, is it really worth the trouble? You will ultimately have to decide that for yourself and whether to embrace this model in your practice after graduation. However, there are good reasons why we believe that you will find this model to be worth emulating.

First, you will find that the time invested in client-centered efforts will actually pay off—that they are cost-effective, even in the lives of such over-worked (and underpaid) lawyers as public defenders and legal services attorneys. Second, you will find that the efforts invested will improve outcomes for your clients; they will result in better-developed and better-implemented client theories. Third, you will find that clients will ultimately be more satisfied with your services; they will recommend their friends to you and they will come back themselves for repeat business.

Finally, although we could list many other benefits of client-centered representation, client-centered representation "feels good." It feels good for you and for your clients. And, that benefit alone should probably be sufficient to encourage you to try on the mantle of client-centered lawyer, even as you critically evaluate its benefits and costs over the course of your clinical experience and throughout your legal career.

Chapter 7
Interviewing

Interviewing? Why should it be necessary to teach you how to interview? You've been interviewed for jobs and you may have interviewed others for employment or even interviewed clients as part of your job. You interview people all the time at parties and other settings to figure out if you want to go out with them or to have them as friends. So, why waste any precious time in your clinical experience learning how to interview?

There are two answers to the basic question of why we spend time on interviewing. First, there is a lot of really horrible interviewing in the world. How many times have you gone through a job interview and left feeling that, at the end of the interview, the interviewer had no real sense of who you were and what you could achieve? Developing oneself into a skilled and effective interviewer will distinguish you from many in the legal community and will help set up the rest of your relationships with clients.

Second, and equally important, although nearly everyone has some experience in interviewing, interviewing for lawyers implicates skills and values that are fundamentally different from those applicable in other settings. As we will see, the goals of the interviewing session should define both the structure of the interviewing session and the techniques used therein.

A. Importance of Interviewing

It is difficult to overstate the importance of good interviewing techniques and values. A "good" interview establishes the foundation for all of the representation activities to come; a "poor" interview creates an obstacle that must be overcome if effective representation is to be provided. While it is not possible to describe a "perfect" interview, it is easy to define an "inadequate" interview. An "inadequate" interview is one that fails on one or both of the following grounds. First, it might so alienate the client or so destroy any rapport or sense of confidence by the client in the lawyer that there is no recovery— the client may not even come back for more. Second, it might provide so little information or such inaccurate information that there is either nothing useful that the lawyer can do before s/he meets with the client again or the lawyer will embark on a course of action that will be contrary to the client's long-term interests. Both of those outcomes can be avoided through the development of effective interviewing skills and values.

B. Goals of Interviewing

Perhaps you remember the old television series "Dragnet" or perhaps you saw the 1987 movie version with Dan Aykroyd and Tom Hanks. In the series, Sergeant Joe Friday would interview witnesses and caution them with the words, "Just the facts, ma'am." And, certainly, "getting the facts" is an important goal of interviewing. However, it is hardly the only goal. And, as we will discover, it must often yield to the realization of other, more urgent goals.

Among the other goals of the interviewing process are:

To establish an appropriate attorney-client relationship

Every client enters the lawyer-client relationship with some expectations about the role that s/he is to play. Often, the client's vision of this role is very different from the role either that the lawyer envisions or that will maximize the likelihood that the client's goals will be achieved. Perhaps the client expects the lawyer to take charge, make all the decisions, and barely consult with the client—a model very different from the client-centered approach we will utilize in clinic.

While the client has the right to define his/her role for him/herself, that definition should be a conscious act on the part of the client. And, ensuring that the decision as to role is a conscious, informed one means that the lawyer must begin to address that issue in the interview. The lawyer must make it clear to the client that whatever models the client may have seen on television or in movies or heard described by friends and relatives, the lawyer would like to build a model in which the client and his/her problems are at the center of the relationship and the lawyer functions as a helper, advisor, and counselor.

To obtain the client's identification of problem

The client may have sought legal assistance at his/her own initiative or at the urging of a family member, friend, court official, or other. Whoever was the moving force in this process, the client believes that there is some problem or set of problems that might be addressed through legal representation. The lawyer in the initial interview must begin to get the client's sense of that problem or problems. However, as we will see, the client's characterization of the problem will only be the beginning of the identification process.

To obtain the client's "story" (description of the "facts")

Although we will not use the term "story" with the client (because it seems to suggest a fictional account), the client is the initial source for our development of the "facts" of the case. As we will discover, these "facts" are hard (and ordinarily impossible) to determine absolutely. However, because we will need to tell a coherent story as part of our "theory of the client," we need to begin somewhere. That somewhere is our client and his/her story.

To obtain the client's identification of goals

Our client will also probably come to the interview with some sense of what s/he hopes to achieve through our legal representation. However, as with other aspects of client representation, this identification of goals will be the beginning of a long process—not necessarily the end. For example, a client may come in with the expressed goal of obtaining a bankruptcy. Through questioning of the client, we may discover that the client's reason for expressing that goal is that creditors have been harassing him/her. The client may also express a desire to extinguish outstanding bills. Therefore, to the extent that we can address the harassment and potentially extinguish those bills, bankruptcy (and its associated disadvantages) may prove unnecessary.

To begin to identify legally relevant witnesses

Our client may also be a source of potential witnesses who might support or undercut her version of the events. We use the term "legally relevant" to refer to these possible witnesses for several reasons. First, since there is probably no "case" at this time, it is impossible to tell which witnesses might testify as to what facts. Second, the witness may never testify him/herself, but may lead us to witnesses who will testify if the case goes to hearing or trial. Third, the witness may provide us with information that will be useful not at trial, but in negotiations or other critical steps in the representation process. So, we will want to be open to a wide range of potential witnesses who may have information about our client or the significant events or who may otherwise assist us in representing our client.

To begin to identify legally relevant documents

In much the same way that we need to be open to a wide range of potential witnesses, so we also need to be open to a wide range of "legally relevant" documents. We cannot limit ourselves to "admissible" documents at this stage because we do not know what documents we might try to admit as exhibits and we do not know at this early stage whether we will be able to meet potential evidentiary objections (*i.e.*, authentication, foundation). Likewise, a document may be very effective in negotiations, even if it would not be admissible in court. Inadmissible documents might also lead to admissible documents. So, we will throw out a wide net for potential documents. And, we will start with documents identified by our client to begin this process.

To evaluate the client as a potential witness

We will only see our client for the first time once. Our perceptions at every interaction after that first interaction will be influenced by what has gone before. That means that you will have only one opportunity to see your client in the way that a judge or jury or opposing counsel will see your client that first time. Since client image is at least malleable and since the value of a client as a witness may be a critical part of evaluating that client's case, this opportunity to evaluate the client as a potential witness is an important goal in the interview.

To create a contractual bond between lawyer and client

Although some state rules of professional conduct still do not require a written retainer between attorney and client, even in those jurisdictions attorneys are strongly encouraged to memorialize the scope of representation in a written document. In other jurisdictions, a written retainer is required before a lawyer is authorized to act on behalf of a client and/or to bill the client for services provided.

Moreover, regardless of the ethical rules, a well-drafted written retainer can facilitate communication between attorney and client. Too often, client expectations about the scope of legal representation are very different from the expectations of the lawyer. The client may believe that the lawyer has committed him/herself to pursue a case up through the United States Supreme Court. By contrast, the lawyer may believe that s/he has simply agreed to investigate client options and to advise the client of those options. The written retainer can help (albeit not guarantee) that the lawyer and client will be working from the same understanding about the nature of their relationship. The written retainer can also help avoid misunderstandings about the responsibility of the client to pay for certain court costs and litigation expenses (even where the client is not being charged for legal services).

So, creating a contractual bond will ordinarily be an important goal of the interviewing process. While the initial interview may be too early a point for the lawyer to know whether s/he wants to provide representation or for the client to know whether s/he wants to have the lawyer represent her/him, at some point during or soon after the initial interview, the client will need to execute a retainer authorizing at least a limited scope of representation to conduct an initial fact investigation, to conduct initial legal research, and to determine what legal assistance might be provided.

To inspire client confidence in the attorney

Trust is an important commodity in the lawyer-client relationship. In order to effectively represent the client, the lawyer must have the client's trust. However, trust is not automatic at the beginning of that relationship. It ordinarily must be earned by the lawyer.

There are two components of trust. First, the client must believe that the lawyer is truly invested in the client and in solving his/her problems. That might be described as the *emotional* component of trust. Second, the client must believe that the lawyer has the capability to effectively represent the client's interests. That might be described as the *substantive* component of trust.

You might be wondering at this point why any client should have confidence in you. The reality is that you will do an excellent job on behalf of your clients. Although you are new to the practice of law, you will be able to focus your energies on the clients you will be representing in clinic. And, although you have not worked as a lawyer before, you will be able to pull from all of the resources (clinical teachers, other students, library resources, etc.) available in clinic. So, think about how you will present these strengths in your initial interviews without feeling a need to be defensive about your lack of experience.

To build rapport between lawyer and client

Rapport is a very different factor from trust and it is also a very different factor from friendship. In building rapport with your clients you will be working to have them know that you care about them and their situations, that you are an empathic or empathetic individual. From this quality, you will work to build a relationship in which the client will want to spend time with you and be open with you about the important things in his/her life.

To protect the client from damaging behavior after the initial interview

By the time that clients come to see you, they may already be embroiled in complex legal disputes. They also have the ability to do untold harm to their situation if they take certain actions without considering the consequences of those actions. For example, they may be contacted by an adverse party or by a representative of that party. Should they talk to that individual? If they should talk, what should they say? Are there actions that they could take to strengthen or weaken their position in a pending dispute? If so, it is critical that those actions and their implications be identified with the client so that the client can make an informed decision about what behaviors to avoid and what behaviors are safe to undertake. Again, the client will make the ultimate decision, but the client needs the information necessary to make an informed decision.

To provide initial counseling to the client

We will discuss counseling as a separate topic later in this text. However, the distinction between counseling and interviewing reflected by their placement in separate chapters in this book belies the fact that clear distinctions are difficult to draw. Although a session between lawyer and client may be labeled "initial interview," the client may want to know what his/her options are and how the lawyer values those options. In a subsequent "counseling" session, the lawyer may frequently obtain additional information in a process that looks an awful lot like interviewing. Therefore, although we will postpone our discussion of counseling for a later chapter, do not be surprised if the client seeks some initial counseling in the interview stages of the relationship. However, at the same time, do not be rushed into evaluating options before you have had a chance to conduct necessary fact investigation and legal research.

C.   Inconsistency of Goals

These many goals of interviewing are not necessarily complementary in the short-term. For example, the goal of creating rapport between lawyer and client through ice-breaking and small talk might take up time in the initial interview at the expense of obtaining a complete story from the client. In the short-term, we may have to sacrifice the realization of one goal for the achievement of another. However, as we will discuss, in the long-term we will discover that these goals are complementary—that the lawyer who builds rapport will ultimately be far more successful in developing the facts and the lawyer who inspires confidence will ultimately be far more successful in furthering client goals.

D.   Techniques and Choices

There are books that teach the techniques of interviewing as if interviewing was a recipe in a cookbook that could be followed again and again to achieve the same results—take one teaspoon of icebreaking, add six open-ended questions, stir in a tablespoon of fact development, then fold in a cup of active listening and the result will be a well-seasoned interview. While such a recipe might be easy to follow, it will give you a false sense of security. Like many patterns, one size often fits nobody. And, checklists will too often get the information you expect, not the information you need.

Many books on interviewing also present "rules" of interviewing—the interviewer should always sit across from the interviewee, the interviewer should always start the interview with ice breaking, the interviewer should always wear a suit. This book rejects that approach and instead focuses on opportunities for choices and the process for making those choices.

This focus is admittedly much more complex than the approach used in other texts. However, it is presented because it ultimately will make you a better interviewer for all of the clients with whom you will interact. And, the choices and techniques discussed in this section will have practical application to the choices we will confront and techniques we will employ in such other stages of the lawyering process as counseling and negotiation.

Let us therefore begin by looking at a fairly simple question—the choice about whether to shake hands with a prospective client at the beginning of the interview. The initial response might be that there is no choice here at all, that the lawyer should always shake the hand of a prospective client. However, like nearly every rule in which the words "always" or "never" appear, we will discover that the answer may not be quite so obvious. Instead, we will find, the correct answer is "it depends."

For example, should a woman attorney shake hands with an older male client? Does it make a difference if the client is an orthodox Jew or comes from a culture in which men and women who are not married to each other do not shake hands? Should a younger male lawyer shake hands with an elderly female client? Perhaps, but is there a risk associated with that decision that must be balanced against the benefit that would likely be achieved by shaking hands?

So, the answer to the "shaking hands question" may be yes, most of the time, and no, some of the time. However, even when we consciously identify the choice and consider the benefits and disadvantages of each option, we may still be left making a decision based on incomplete facts and therefore inadequate predictive outcomes. At those times, we are left with the risk-benefit matrix (discussed in chapter two) to avoid choices that are high risk and minimum benefit. And, we are reminded of the need to learn as much as we can about the world (like the impact of different cultural norms) to bring into our lawyering.

The decision about what to wear to an interview is a similarly complex issue that appears to be deceptively simple. You have all of those suits that you have bought or that your family may have bought for you. Surely, you might as well get some use out of them for more than interviewing season. Well, what will be the impact on your client of having you meet him/her in a dark suit? Is there a risk that the client may be intimidated or distanced? Possibly, but especially so if the client is not used to dealing with lawyers and expects the lawyer to direct the attorney-client relationship. Is there an image that you may want to create in the client's mind about your professionalism as evidenced in your attire? Probably you do, but this will be especially true if you are somewhat young and the client is a business client used to dealing with contemporaries in three-piece suits.

Again, we may have to make our choice with incomplete information about our prospective client and with inadequate predictors of the likely outcome of various choices. We might err on the side of formality, feeling that the benefit of professionalism outweighs the risk of increased distance between lawyer and client. We might try to split the difference and wear a blazer and slacks or a skirt in order to present a professional image with a lower intimidation factor. Whatever the choice we make, our choice will have certain inherent risks and will trade-off particular benefits.

E. Stages

Although every interview is different, there are ordinarily certain stages that most interviews include. However, although these stages are presented in a chronological order in this text, even if the interview includes all of these stages, it may not develop in such a linear manner. The more important thing to consider is that in most interviews you will need to address the goals identified with each of these stages.

1. Background Research

It is seldom necessary to do factual or legal research in order to conduct an excellent interview. However, there may be occasions when some research in advance of the interview will be helpful. For example, if you know the legal problem for which the client is seeking assistance and if that area of the law is unfamiliar to you, you may wish to learn something about that area. Likewise, if your client is involved in an activity or area of business that you know little about, you may wish to learn something about that activity or area in order to facilitate rapport with the client and in order to communicate interest in the client and his/her concerns.

At the same time, a little research can be a very dangerous thing. A lawyer who learns that a client is seeking assistance with a bankruptcy may learn about the basic substance and procedure of bankruptcy law before the interview. However, that lawyer is more likely to then treat the client as a "bankruptcy case" and to conduct the interview with a focus on bankruptcy.

The danger is that bankruptcy may be the last legal option that the client should pursue and yet the lawyer may start down that road all too easily.

In the clinic context, you may think you know nothing that will be of assistance to a client. The reality, however, is that you know a lot about the law already from your law school experiences in and out of the classroom. And, you also know a lot about life that you bring to your lawyering from your life during and before law school. Together, these two elements of your knowledge will prove to be all you need to know to conduct an outstanding interview with nearly all clients.

2.   Small Talk or Ice-Breaking

Lawyers will ordinarily introduce the interview process in two ways. First, they will engage in some small talk (or "ice-breaking") to relax the client and to begin to establish some rapport. Second, they will provide some foundation for the client regarding the lawyer-client relationship and the interview process that will be utilized that day.

Ice-breaking can take at least two forms. Client-non-specific ice-breaking ordinarily includes comments like, "Did you have any problems finding the office?" or "Nice weather we've been having." These are comments that could be used in nearly any kind of interaction with nearly any kind of client. By contrast, client-specific ice-breaking includes interactions that are specific to this client—using information that might have been obtained when the interview was arranged or that is public knowledge. This might include remarks related to a client's employment or family.

Although we tend to look upon small talk as a transitional phase before we "get down to business," it can serve at least two more important purposes. First, small talk can elicit relevant information that will be critical to addressing the problems for which the client is seeking assistance. Often information is obtained in this stage that transforms the entire interview. Second, small talk can establish a rhythm for the attorney-client relationship—a conversational rhythm of give and take between lawyer and client. In this way, ice-breaking may help break down hierarchical barriers separating lawyer and client and may encourage the client to treat the interview more as a conversation and less as a cross-examination characterized by narrow, leading questions and brief, controlled responses.

So, should small talk *always* be a part of the interview process? Well, the word "always" should be a tip-off that the answer is "it depends." For example, some clients will come into the interview process with a desperate, urgent need to get their problem off their chest. In such a case, it is critical that the lawyer pick up on clues from the client. The lawyer may then choose to eliminate (or at least postpone) the ice-breaking stage until the client has a chance to "come clean" or "get it off his/her chest." Again, there is no absolute right answer to the decision to engage in small talk, only a choice that must be made on the spot based on the best information available to the lawyer.

3. Introduction or Foundation

Often a lawyer will introduce the interview process with an explanation of what the lawyer hopes to achieve in the interview and the process that the lawyer hopes to utilize to achieve those goals. This will ordinarily be presented to the client in tentative language ("This is what I hope to do today in our initial interview. Does that sound okay?"). The lawyer may also address such parameters for the interview as the amount of time the client and lawyer have available, any fees for the initial consultation, and such concerns as confidentiality and the attorney-client privilege.

In the clinic context, there are other foundational issues that will ordinarily need to be addressed. To reduce the risk of misunderstandings about the unauthorized practice of law, a student attorney will ordinarily briefly explain his/her status under the student practice rule (if applicable) and the basic operation of the clinic. Clients may not fully understand fee arrangements, if any, and the role of the clinical supervisor (since in most clinics the supervisor does not sit in on client interviews). The goal here is to explain the nature of the clinic and the student's status in a non-defensive way (not, "I know that you wish you could afford a 'real' lawyer, but instead you've got me."), but one that is accurate (in part to avoid any questions about misrepresentation or unauthorized practice of law). Think about how you will explain your role in advance of your initial interview. It is a difficult concept to explain off the top of your head.

Many lawyers will tell you that you must explain the issues of confidentiality and attorney-client privilege at the beginning of every interview. However, like other issues we have looked at, there are no hard and fast rules here. Explanation of the attorney-client privilege may be necessary to facilitate communication. However, it is very difficult to explain confidentiality accurately *and* briefly. Thus, one runs the risk of turning the introduction or foundation stage into a monologue by the lawyer with the client only indicating that s/he understands what the lawyer is saying (even if s/he does not). That will have an extremely negative effect on the rhythm of the rest of the interview; it will tend to make the client extremely passive. So, like many things, a little foundation will go a long way.

This is especially significant since, as a general rule, clients will err on the side of giving too little information, rather than too much. They are often afraid of "wasting" the lawyer's time (even if they are paying for the initial interview) and/or of running on too long and appearing foolish. Since too much information is seldom a problem for a lawyer and too little information is usually a ticket for disaster, you need to provide an indication to the client early on that the conversation (hopefully established through small talk) should continue throughout the interview—that what is desired is a dialogue and not a monologue.

4.   Overview

In the overview stage, we hope to get a sense of the client's problem(s), the client's story (or stories), and the client's identification of goals for the legal representation. This stage might be described as the "big picture" stage—the stage at which we try to get a general sense of our client, his/her social and legal environment, his/her hopes for our legal assistance, and the nature of the problems and underlying facts that brought him/her to seek our help.

The overview stage is a process that will ordinarily be characterized by the use of open-ended questions—questions designed to elicit narrative answers from the client. Usually, these open-ended questions will be structured to guide the client into providing us with a chronological story—"Once upon a time there was a . . . ." "And then a dragon appeared on the scene and . . . ." "And then I slew the dragon and . . . ." "And now the owners of the dragon are seeking . . . ." "And so, I need your help to live happily ever after."

Often the chronological development of a story is easier said than done. Some clients are unable to tell a narrative in a coherent, chronological manner. That will be important for us to know as we evaluate the client as a potential witness. Some stories may not lend themselves to a tidy, chronological development. However, attempting to elicit the story chronologically is ordinarily the place to start in developing the "big picture."

5.   Development of Initial Theories of the Client

As we begin to develop the "big picture" with the client, it is only natural that we will begin to think about particular aspects of the client's story in legal and non-legal terms. The client's description of physical and mental abuse at the hands of a domestic partner may lead us to think about domestic violence laws and procedures. While this is natural and almost unavoidable, there are several reasons why it is important to recognize the risks of locking oneself too soon into any concrete theories (or strategies) for the client.

First, we know so little about the client at this stage that it is impossible to know whether a particular theory (or approach) will actually further the client's interests. Second, we know so little about the nature of the underlying facts and law at this stage that it is dangerous to focus on a theory that ultimately may not "fly." Third, a preoccupation with one theory may lead us to ignore or to fail to fully develop other theories that could ultimately be far more beneficial to the client. Fourth, it is not our role as the lawyer to make decisions about or between alternative theories for the client. We will need to develop sufficient information to maximize the opportunity for the client to make an informed decision between alternative theories—whether these theories are complementary or mutually exclusive.

And yet, despite these risks, there are good reasons why we want to brainstorm creatively as the client's story is presented. As we think about the client's story, certain options may come to mind that require the development of more facts. Although we should resist the temptation to interrupt the client's story to develop these facts (at least until we have the "big picture"), we will need to develop these facts at some point—in this interview if time permits or in a later interview or through an independent fact investigation. As we think about the client's story, certain options may come to mind that require legal research. Again, although we should resist the temptation to interrupt the client's story to conduct that research, we will need to conduct that legal research at some point.

6.   Fact Development

After we obtain the "big picture," we will need to fill in a lot of the gaps. In a very real sense, it is like the old television game show "Concentration." A puzzle was placed on a screen and covered up by 30 numbered squares. Over the course of the game, these numbered squares were removed, two at a time, and more and more of the puzzle was displayed. However, while the game was in progress, all one could often discern was a mass of squiggly lines.

In the interview process, we are trying to develop facts that fill in the missing pieces of the puzzle—that flesh out the missing or inconsistent or ambiguous portions of the client's story. And, although it may seem counterintuitive, we will try to develop these facts whether they support or weaken the various theories that we might have begun to develop for the client. We need to know what's out there to undercut various approaches as well as to support particular strategies.

Whereas the overview stage was characterized by open-ended questions, we are likely to make more use of narrow directed questions in this stage. We might ask: "You mentioned that this happened, were there any other persons present?" "Did you lose any days of work because of the accident?" We may even use leading questions, although usually as a last resort, when necessary to nail down or confirm particular points that we think we understood from the client's story.

If we think about the overview stage as an effort to develop a story a mile wide and an inch deep, in the fact development stage we will be digging deeply—to take the big picture that we developed in the overview stage and fill in the details. Within the time and other constraints applicable, we will use this stage to begin to develop the facts that will create a body from the skeleton of the overview.

7.   Conclusion

In this stage, there are at least five basic tasks that will ordinarily need to be accomplished. First, if the client is ready to retain us (and if we are ready to be retained for at least further investigation and evaluation of options), a retainer will need to be signed to authorize us to take additional steps on behalf of the client. Second, if further investigation requires the review of personal records that must be obtained by the lawyer (*i.e.*, medical records, education records, social welfare records), the client will need to sign authorizations for release of these records.

Third, the lawyer will ordinarily need to outline plans for the future—"I will call you next week. In the meantime, I will be conducting the following fact investigation . . . and will be conducting research on the following legal issues . . . ." Fourth, the lawyer and client will have to divide up those additional responsibilities that the client will need to take on—bringing in documents in the possession of the client, having the client obtain records from third parties in order to not put those parties on notice of the involvement of the lawyer, telling friends that the lawyer will be contacting them and asking those friends to cooperate.

Fifth, since one of the goals of the interview is to protect the client from damaging behavior, the lawyer and client will need to discuss any issues of concern that have been identified during the interview. For example, in a collection case, the lawyer and client may want to discuss how the client should respond to calls from collection agency representatives. In a personal injury case, the lawyer and client may want to discuss how the client should respond to settlement proposals by an insurance company claims representative.

8.   Ordering our Stages

Although these stages are presented in a linear manner (1. Background research → 2. Introduction → 3. Overview → 4. Theory of the client development → 5. Fact development → 6. Conclusion), few interviews actually develop in such a neat linear (1 → 2 → 3 → 4 → 5 → 6) manner. For example, as facts are developed in stage five, new theories often come to mind and these theories will then require the development of more facts. Such an interview might develop as 1 → 2 → 3 → 4 → 5 → 4 → 5 → 4 → 5 → 6.

Or, a client who comes in with a desperate need to "spit out" his/her story might dictate an interview pattern that looks like 3 (Overview) → 4 (Theory of the client development) → 2 (Introduction) → 5 (Fact development) → 4 (Theory of the client development) → 5 (Fact development) → 6 (Closure). Even then, the notion that stages are necessarily discrete and separable ignores the reality of most interviews. So, instead, look upon the stages as guidance for the goals that need to be achieved in the interview process and the ways in which those goals will ordinarily be achieved.

F.   Non-Verbal Communication

While we often tend of think about interviewing in terms of the words that are exchanged between lawyer and client, words are only part of the tools of communication that are critical to effective interviewing. Among the non-verbal factors that must be mastered are "proxemics," "kinesics," "paralinguistics," and "chronemics."

1.   Proxemics

The term "proxemics" refers to the impact of spatial relationships on communication. Where should a lawyer sit in relation to the client in the interview? Should the lawyer sit across from the client? Should the lawyer sit next to the client or kitty-corner to the client? Although most lawyers sit directly across from their clients with their desks serving as a barrier, that is certainly not the only option and may not be the best option for a specific lawyer interviewing a specific client.

For example, a younger woman attorney interviewing an older male business client may wish to utilize the most formal interviewing structure (client and lawyer separated by a desk) to anticipate client expectations and to use that formality to increase her credibility as an attorney. Like other choices in the lawyering process, we must ask, "What is the potential benefit of a particular interviewing structure and what is the potential risk associated with that structure?" And, like other choices, we will rely on research and life experiences to make that assessment, but we will always acknowledge that we cannot have all the information necessary to make a completely informed decision.

2. Kinesics

Kinesics or "body language" refers to the use of body movements (or the failure to move) as a communications device. Nodding of the head, gesturing with the hand, leaning forward with the body, all involve body movements that can communicate particular information to the client. And, they can often communicate information to the client in ways that words cannot.

For example, a client narrating his/her story in the classic "overview" stage will often look to the lawyer for guidance about how long to go on. Clients, in the main, are concerned about running on too long and either wasting the lawyer's time or appearing foolish to the lawyer. They will therefore often look to the lawyer for information about how to tell the story.

A lawyer who maintains eye contact with the client and who nods his/her head occasionally will usually communicate to the client that s/he is taking in the client's story and that the client should continue telling it. Likewise, writing down notes from the client's story will often be interpreted by clients as valuing the information that the client is relating. The danger here is that if the lawyer writes something down at one point and fails to write something down at another point, the client may interpret the failure to write as indicating that that information is not valuable to the lawyer. The taking of notes then becomes a powerful, albeit ambiguous, "prompt" for the client.

3. Paralinguistics

Paralinguistics refers to the use of such vocal phenomena as pace, pitch, tone, and volume as a communications device. The impact of such phenomena may be much more powerful than the actual content of the lawyer's speech. The lawyer may slow down his/her speech for emphasis, may increase the pitch to communicate excitement, may lower the tone to communicate seriousness, or may increase or decrease the volume to draw client attention.

4. Chronemics

Chronemics refers to the timing of communications. In an interview there may be topics that are embarrassing to discuss. To the extent that the lawyer has a choice about when to raise such topics, it is ordinarily better to address these topics later in the interviewing process—after a level of trust has been established between attorney and client—rather than early in the process when there is less reason for the client to be honest with the lawyer.

5. Personal Appearance

Fashion designers would have us believe that we are what we wear. While most of us would agree that that is an overstatement, the way we dress does communicate information about us to the client. If we are not clean, if we are disheveled, if we are dressed in a way that our clients do not associate with "professional" demeanor, our clients may conclude that we are not likely to provide them with effective services.

Our office surroundings can also tell our clients a great deal about us. An office that is disorganized and that has files strewn everywhere may be interpreted by a client to mean that we are also disorganized in our work. In addition, files left strewn around may suggest to a client that we are not scrupulous about maintaining client confidentiality.

Admittedly, such client perceptions are based on stereotypes. However, these stereotypes are very powerful and the initial interview may not be the time to try to challenge them. Instead, it is usually far better to acknowledge their power and to accommodate them during those initial client contacts.

G. Acknowledging our Limitations

Student attorneys often feel betrayed when they discover during the course of the attorney-client relationship that their clients either did not pour out their entire life story to them during the initial interview or that the story has changed over the course of the attorney-client relationship. While we always need to accept the fact that we may have gotten it wrong to begin with, there are also several factors to keep in mind that can inhibit the client from telling the "full" story in those initial contacts.

Like most human beings, the client may consciously or unconsciously tell her/his story in a way to minimize threats to her/his ego—to make her/himself appear better than s/he behaved during the critical events. Or, the client may "spin" her/his story in order to minimize facts that the client believes will harm her/his case. The client may also revise her/his story to conform to social norms; s/he may not reveal critical details to someone of a different race or gender or age.

Since time for interviews is seldom unlimited, competing time demands may lead the client to focus his/her story on the facts that s/he believes are important. The physical environment of being in a lawyer's office or in a setting that is culturally or economically uncomfortable may also impede communication between lawyer and client. Moreover, most people will try to avoid discussing events that were traumatic. Finally, memory may simply fail. The client may remember more information or may remember information differently in succeeding interactions.

Despite our ability to rationally understand that memory is imperfect and that trust is not automatic, we often feel a powerful sense of betrayal when information does not develop as we believed and hoped it would. These feelings are often even more powerful when we are just starting out as lawyers and our professional identities and reputations seem so fragile. However, even with the best interviewing techniques, these problems are likely to occur and all we can do is grapple with our feelings and not let them interfere with our relationships with our clients.

H. Minimizing the Harm

There are other things we can do to minimize the effects of these inhibiting factors. But, all of these compensating techniques depend on us intensively listening to our clients and observing their non-verbal clues. Like many other lawyering tasks, interviewing can be a physically and mentally exhausting task.

Part of our listening will be directed at client questions and responses. When we ask a question, does the client answer it in full or only in part? A partial response may be an indication that there is more there to talk about. However, for reasons of chronemics, we may make a note to ourselves about this issue and wait to pursue it further at a later date. An even more powerful indication of a potentially troublesome issue is a non-response by the client. The client may answer a question other than the one we asked or may avoid the question entirely. Here we must also always be mindful that our questions may not be as artfully crafted as we think. That may be the cause of the client's perceived avoidance of our questions rather than any action on the part of the client.

There are other factors that can increase your ability to get the maximum accurate information from your clients—at least as your clients understand the information to be accurate. You can be explicit about the benefits of getting the "whole story"—making clear the extrinsic reward of "coming clean." You can focus on the cathartic benefits of telling the story, of "getting it off your chest." These and other benefits can increase the client's willingness to talk without reservation.

I.   Constructing our Clients

To a very significant extent, we "construct" our own clients. A client interviewed by one lawyer may behave very differently when interviewed by another attorney. One lawyer may describe a client as forthcoming and honest while another lawyer may describe the same client as withdrawn and dishonest. The difference is not in the client, although clients can have better or worse days; the difference is in the signals that the lawyer has sent to the client and the ways that the client has responded to those signals. We "construct" our own clients by our interviewing techniques.

Compounding this phenomenon is the impact of attorney gap-filling— filling in the gaps in client stories ourselves rather than by seeking additional information from our clients. Too often we will make guesses about the meaning to be given to certain actions based on our experiences and our application of those experiences to interpretations of client actions. That is common human behavior. However, it is fraught with dangers. Too often our experiential background may not comport with the experiences of our clients. And, even if our experiences are generally the same, the specific experiences in this case may not comport with our more general reality.

Our tendency is to fit our clients and their stories into neat packages. So, be conscious of the role that we play as lawyers in constructing our clients— for better and for worse.

J.   Special Ethical Issues

An ethical issue that arises in some interviews is whether the attorney should discuss the law with the client before or after getting facts from the client? Among the ethical rules implicated here is Rule 3.3 of the ABA

Model Rules of Professional Conduct (2000-2001). This rule provides as follows:

> (a)   A lawyer shall not knowingly:
>
> > (1)   make a false statement of material fact or law to a tribunal;
> >
> > (2)   fail to disclose a material fact to a tribunal when disclosure is necessary to avoid assisting a criminal or fraudulent act by the client;
> >
> > * * *
> >
> > (4)   offer evidence that the lawyer knows to be false. If a lawyer has offered material evidence and comes to know of its falsity, the lawyer shall take reasonable remedial measures.

Rule 3.4 similarly prohibits a lawyer from "assist[ing] a witness to testify falsely . . . ."

If we tell our client about the "law" first, we run the risk of having the client alter his/her story to fit the legal requirements. A client charged with murder who is informed about the impact of mental state on the various degrees of homicide may embellish his mental state to fit the law. However, by avoiding directly "coaching" a client on his/her story, the lawyer may not "know" that the client has altered his story to fit the law. Since the ethical standard deals with "knowingly" taking certain acts, we will have stayed on the side of the angels.

But, will we have really stopped short of the ethical divide? Mightn't we "know" in our heart of hearts that our client's diminished capacity really came from his/her understanding of the law and not from an honest recounting of the facts? Mightn't we "know" that our client has adapted his/her "story" to fit within the parameters of a legal excuse?

At the same time, wouldn't a policy that forbade lawyers from sharing legal analysis with their clients ultimately punish exactly the wrong class of clients? Those clients who are sophisticated in the law (and who could tailor their stories) would be rewarded at the expense of those clients who are naïve about the law (and who might not understand the significance of certain facts within their stories). Moreover, shouldn't a client be able to ask his/her lawyer for an analysis of the law in order to make an informed decision?

Ultimately, it will come down to how much the attorney wants and needs to know about the client's version of the facts before proceeding. Certainly the lawyer cannot ethically present testimony that s/he "knows" to be false. But there is "knowing" and there is *knowing*. And while many criminal attorneys explicitly tell their clients that they do not want to know whether or not they committed the crime with which they are charged, they will need to know everything that the prosecution can put forward to make a case against their client. Some of that information will initially come from their client through such questions as, "What will the State say about you in order to convict you?"

There is no consensus among lawyers as to where to precisely draw the ethical line in coaching clients. Within a fairly wide continuum of lawyer decisions, different lawyers will therefore make different choices about the extent to which they will or will not "coach" their clients about the law. You will ultimately have to decide where you will draw the line within the range of settings you will confront.

Chapter 8
Fuzzy Thinking

During the 2000 Presidential Campaign, then-candidate George Bush's positions on tax relief and spending were criticized by Vice President Al Gore during a televised debate. Governor Bush responded by attacking Gore's analysis as "fuzzy math." The phrase "fuzzy math" became a buzzword during the campaign for "wrong-headedness." And, the mere mention of the phrase effectively shut off further debate.

That use of the adjective "fuzzy" hearkens back for many of us to our days in high school or college. Perhaps we received a lower than anticipated grade on an essay accompanied by the comments: "Turgid prose and fuzzy thinking." So, if we were being criticized for thinking "fuzzy," "fuzzy thinking" must be a bad thing, mustn't it?

We will discover that "fuzziness" can actually be a good quality and one that we will want to encourage in our lawyering. However, we will approach the concept of fuzzy thinking as meaning something very different from vague or unclear or imprecise thinking—the way that term is frequently used. Instead, fuzzy thinking will be something to strive towards in order to achieve results that cannot be achieved through traditional thinking.

A. Defining our Terms

So, what is fuzzy thinking? Fuzzy thinking is a form of reasoning based on the use of "fuzzy," as opposed to "crisp," sets. A "crisp" set is a set in which something is or is not a member. A "fuzzy" set is a set in which members of the set are not simply "in or out," but rather are members to a degree. The concept is one that we borrow from the fields of mathematics, electrical engineering, linguistics, and logic. But, don't tune out yet.

Think, for example, about a client who has been involved in an automobile accident. The client describes a witness as a "tall" man. Without hearing any more (and without asking any additional questions), we have conjured up an image in our mind of that "tall" man—we have "gap filled" his characteristics. We even have an image of how tall that "tall" man is based on our experiences. But, is that definition of "tallness" the same as that of our client?

In America today, the average man is 5'9" tall. We might therefore define a "tall" man as anyone taller than the average—taller than 5'9". That is an example of a "crisp" definition of tallness. A man who is 5'10" would be tall; a man who is 6'0" would be tall; a man who is 6'4" would be tall. All of these men would be "in" the "crisp" set of "tall" men because each man is taller than our benchmark of 5'9"; each would be a 100% member of the "crisp" set of "tall" men.

But, as we know, there are significant differences in the degrees of tallness between the three men described above. "Fuzzy" thinking recognizes these differences by providing individuals with a degree of membership in the "fuzzy" set of "tall" men. A man who is 5'10" tall is taller than the average man, but is not a strong member of the fuzzy set of tall men. We might assign to him a degree of fuzzy membership of 60%. A man who is 6'0" tall would be a stronger member of the fuzzy set of tall men, perhaps an 80% member, but would not be as strong a member as a man who is 6'4" tall (who might be a 90% member).

Saying that an individual is tall in a "crisp" system tells us little about that individual's tallness. All we know is that the individual is at least as tall as our prototype "tall" individual. By contrast, an individual's degree of membership in the "fuzzy" set of tall people gives us a real sense of the relative "tallness" of that person. We know both the benchmark of "tallness" and the relative "tallness" of individuals compared to that benchmark and to each other.

B. Variability of Language

As is probably obvious by now, the characteristics of a "fuzzy" definition of set membership (or of a "crisp" definition), like such characteristics as "beauty," vary with the eye of the beholder. Each of us has a prototype in mind based on our experiences—affected by such factors as race, culture, gender, age, socio-economic status, and sexual orientation. An Inuit client, for example, may have a very different definition of "coldness" in mind than a client from Nigeria.

Fuzzy thinking also constantly reminds us of the variability of language—that a native of Fiji might have a very different image in mind when she uses the word "house" than might a native of the Bronx or a native of Finland. And, by reminding us of the variability of language—that one person's set of "houses" may be very different from another person's set of "houses"—

we will be constantly reminded of the dangers of filling in those definitions based on our own experiences. We will catch ourselves when we start to fill in the "gaps" in our clients' stories; we will avoid taking anything for granted.

The tendency to fill "gaps" in our clients' stories is both universal and powerful. However, each of us fills gaps in our own image based on our own experiences, our own values, and our own culture. When a partner refers to a parent, we conjure up a flesh-and-blood image of that individual without even the benefit of a photograph. When a client refers to a building or a car, we need to resist the impulse to paint the rest of the picture for ourselves. In order to be an effective interviewer, we must get our clients and our other witnesses to fill in the gaps for us, lest our picture not comport with their reality.

C. Fuzzy Client Theory

Fuzzy thinking has obvious application to such lawyering tasks as client interviewing and interviewing of witnesses. However, fuzzy thinking also can help us be more effective lawyers with regard to other lawyering skills and values.

Students often come in early in a criminal defense clinic after having interviewed their client asking, "How can I represent this client? This case is a cold loser!" Or, a student attorney in a civil clinic may come back after an initial interview in a custody case declaring, "This case is a cold winner. This parent is a great client."

Both viewpoints are dangerous and misleading. In criminal cases, few defendants constitute the "perfect" criminal defendant—the defendant who is a 100 percent member of the fuzzy set of "guilty" individuals. Like the Sesame Street sequence that "One of these things is not like the other," there are nearly always things that don't quite fit in the client's picture. In our defense, we will need to concentrate on emphasizing the things that don't fit with the picture of "guilt."

We will begin by identifying the potential factfinder's prototype criminal defendant. Once that prototype is identified, we can then focus on the circumstances of our particular criminal defendant that don't fit that prototype. We will then focus on maximizing the presentation of facts about our client that do not fit that prototype while downplaying or minimizing the facts that make our client closer to a 100 percent member of the fuzzy set of criminal defendants.

We may be representing a client charged with reckless driving. Five minutes before our client was pulled over, the client stopped at a crosswalk to allow a parent to push a baby stroller across the street. The fact that our client stopped to allow a parent and child to cross does not mean that the client was not driving recklessly five minutes later. However, it is a behavioral event that doesn't quite fit with our picture of the prototype "reckless driver"—with the 100 percent member of the fuzzy set of "reckless drivers." We will then play up that evidence in our case theory.

We will also need to be mindful of the clients who seem to be strong members of a fuzzy set that furthers our case theory—the parent who seems to be a very strong member of the fuzzy set of "perfect parents." Few individuals are perfectly good and we need to identify the characteristics and behaviors of our client that do not fit the prototype fuzzy set of "perfect parents." We will then have to anticipate attacks based on those dissonant characteristics and behaviors and to prepare to minimize the aspects of our client that do not fit in the prototype.

D. Applying the Concept in Practice

A student team came into my office rather depressed after their initial client interview. They had just interviewed a high school student who had been expelled from high school for carrying a knife to school. The school district had a "zero tolerance" policy for students carrying knives and the student admitted that he had a knife in his pocket. Any student carrying a knife had to be expelled for one year. The case was an open and shut loser, they declared.

We brought the case back to rounds that day. The team members presented the case and expressed their joint frustration at having no arguments to make. One student in the class asked whether there was a right to a hearing. Yes, the students answered, there was an opportunity for an initial hearing before the assistant principal of the school and an opportunity for a further review by the Board of Education. But, the team member pointed out, the assistant principal and the school board had no discretion under the policy if they found the student was carrying a knife.

"Couldn't you argue something equivalent to jury nullification," one student asked, "that although there appeared to be no discretion, the assistant principal could be persuaded to nullify, to refuse to apply, a policy that seemed overly harsh here?" "Well," I replied, "why does the policy seem too harsh here? Or, phrasing it differently, what about this student does not seem to fit with the prototypical 'knife-carrying student'?"

The team members looked at each other and explained that before the interview, based on their reading of the file, they had a preconception of a "knife-carrying student"—someone out of a modern version of "West Side Story." By contrast, when they met the student, he turned out to be a "good" kid. I then asked, "What was it that made him a "good" kid?"

"What about the fact that this kid is working?" another student asked. "My prototype image of a student carrying a knife to school does not include a student who is actually responsible and works a job outside of school." "It's interesting you raise that," one of the team members said, "the client even indicated that his boss, a pharmacist, would come and testify for him if there's a hearing." "That's another fact that doesn't seem to fit in with this case," the student said. "Knife-carrying students bring up images of gang members and I don't associate gang members getting bosses, especially professionals, to support them." "Gee," said the other team member, "that seems to give us another possible opening."

Another student, an African-American student, asked about the race of the student and the race of the pharmacist. One team member responded that the student was black and the pharmacist was white. "But, what relevance does that have here?" the team member asked." "Well," the student responded, "Doesn't it counter expectations even more to find a *white* pharmacist willing to go out of his way for a *black* high school student?"

"I was wondering," one clinic student asked, "What kind of knife was the student carrying? My image is of a student carrying a switchblade or a buck knife." "No," one of the team members answered, "he was carrying a box knife*—a knife he had used at work to cut up cardboard boxes." "Well, that kind of a knife is a pretty weak member of the fuzzy set of knives, can't we make something of that?" the student continued. "Maybe we can argue that the knife doesn't even fit the legal definition of a knife," a team member added. "Or, we can at least hit on the ways that this knife doesn't fit the image of a knife to be used to hurt another student."

As rounds progressed we began to put more flesh on the bones of the "good" kid and began to identify more and more aspects of the case that didn't seem to "fit." The student attended church; "good" kids might attend church, but prototype "bad" kids don't attend church. The student got solid, albeit not spectacular, grades in school; "good" kids might care about school, but prototype "bad" kids couldn't care less about school. And, on and on we went.

What is largely absent from this episode is any real discussion of "the law." Instead the focus is on telling a story about the student using our "fuzzy

---

* This discussion took place long before the events of September 11, 2001. The use of box knives by several of the terrorists in the airplane hijackings is a powerful reminder that prototypes are not static. And, those events also remind us that all cases take place within a socio-political context.

thinking" approach, a story that would turn factfinder expectations on their head. The ultimate product of this brainstorming was a hearing room full of witnesses—a pharmacist, a minister, a sports coach, family members, and others—all willing to testify about some dimension of our client that made him a "good" kid and not one deserving of expulsion. The ultimate outcome of the hearing was a short suspension of the student, rather than an expulsion, and an interim placement of the student in an alternative high school, a placement that the student attorneys had cleared in advance of the hearing.

E. Fuzzy Thinking in a Bivalent Legal System

Our current legal system is largely bivalent or "crisp" in its approaches. Criminal defendants are either guilty or not guilty of criminal acts; the legal system does not explicitly care about their degree of membership in a "fuzzy" set of guilty individuals. Drivers are either negligent or not negligent (except in those states using comparative negligence). The legal system does not explicitly care about their degree of membership in a "fuzzy" set of negligent drivers.

Even within this bivalent legal system, fuzzy thinking can provide a potentially useful, consistent and unifying conceptual framework for the performance of lawyering tasks. Fuzzy thinking can allow us to argue for discretion in the decision to prosecute in criminal cases by demonstrating how our clients deviate from the prototype criminal. Fuzzy thinking can also allow us to argue for discretion in sentencing in much the same way.

As indicated by the case rounds involving the student who was threatened with expulsion, from "fuzzy thinking" a mighty strategy can be developed. And, from "fuzzy thinking" a mighty strategy can be implemented.

Chapter 9
Collaboration

Think back to your report card in Kindergarten. (Oh, and let's be honest in our recollections.) Did you ever receive an "I"—"Needs Improvement"—as your grade for the evaluative standard "Plays Well With Others"? Did you share your toys with others or did you bite other children when they attempted to "work" with you in the sandbox? And did you collaborate with other children in building blocks or, as indicated in this cartoon, fail to collaborate effectively?

"Norman won't collaborate."

Clinic has its parallels to your work in kindergarten those many years ago. Many of you will work in teams to assist your clinic clients; you will collaborate with another student (or other students). However, even if you are assigned to work alone with your clients, you will be collaborating with your clients in the clinic workspace with other students, in rounds with your clinic colleagues, and in supervision with your clinic supervisor(s).

Many of us, however, got where we are because we refused to share "our toys." We cared a great deal about the quality of our work and we were not about to allow some other child to muck around with our work product. And, why should we change that approach now?

A. Two Heads Are Better Than One

The empirical research on collaboration is strong and growing. When two individuals collaborate, they can bring each partner's strengths to the table and compensate for each other's weaknesses. This has a measurable effect on improving the work product produced by the team beyond that which could be produced alone by either team member.

Collaboration also allows a team to bring the life experiences of both team members to bear on a client's problem. As we have already discovered in interviewing, the broader the range of our life experiences, the more effective we can be as an advocate for a client. Even persons from similar backgrounds have different life experiences. Collaboration makes these differences strengths in the attorney-client relationship.

Collaboration also has documented positive effects on motivation. Because you are working with a partner, someone whom you will not want to let down and someone with whom you will have to share your work progress, motivation is ordinarily even higher for team members than for individuals working alone.

Collaboration also has positive effects on reducing anxiety. The littlest issues, like what to wear to a meeting with a client, can be the source of significant anxiety. The ability to talk options through with another student can significantly alleviate anxiety, especially for those issues that you may wish to discuss first with someone other than your clinical supervisor.

B. Two Heads Are Not Always Better Than One

Although collaboration has positive documented benefits, these benefits are not completely one-sided. Some research has documented circumstances in which collaboration has had a negative effect. It is important therefore to keep these possible disadvantages in mind in order to keep collaboration beneficial.

One downside of collaboration is the creation of some inefficiencies in representation. Not everything can or should be done by all members of a team. In these situations, the need will arise to share or relay information from one team member to another. This may seem like a waste of time. However, the process of sharing information often helps the "reporting" team member see facts and law in a new and different way and provides an opportunity for the "receiving" team member to ask questions and raise issues that the first team member may not have thought of on his/her own.

There is also some research, especially regarding behaviors in incidents like the Cuban missile crisis, which indicates that team members will sometimes engage in behaviors collectively that they would not engage in alone. In these cases, there is the possibility of degraded ethical standards. "If my partner is willing to do this," each member thinks, "then it can't be that bad." Collaborators need to be conscious of this potential effect and vigilant about the fulfillment of ethical responsibilities.

There is also the potential for gridlock in decisionmaking. Especially with a two-person team, it is inevitable that team members will at some point on some issue favor different options. The ability to work those issues through and avoid relying on a clinical supervisor to "break the tie" can require a strong commitment to the collaborative process.

C. Collaboration as a Skill and Value

In the MacCrate Report (discussed in Chapter 1), the Task Force identified "Developing Systems and Procedures for Effectively Working with Other People" as a necessary skill for today's lawyers. Skill 9.4(a) explicitly emphasized the importance of effectively "[c]ollaborating with other attorneys in the same office or other offices."

The vision of the sole practitioner working alone on behalf of his/her clients is being confined more and more these days to black-and-white movies like "Young Abe Lincoln." Lawyers must now often work with in-house counsel in corporations or government agencies, with lawyers in other practices, and with lawyers in their own firms or other settings. Lawyers must learn to work effectively in these collaborative settings.

However, collaboration is also a value that is inescapably intertwined with collaboration as a value. If collaboration is not valued by the members of the team, they will not invest fully in the collaborative process. They will not invest fully in the collaborative process if they do not see benefits. They will not see benefits if they are not good at collaborating. They will not be good at collaborating if they do not understand the characteristics underlying effective collaboration and do not invest in the process.

D. What Is Collaboration?

Before we turn to the characteristics that make for effective collaboration, it is important to develop some common terminology to describe collaboration. Collaboration is more than working together on a case or project. Instead, it envisions a process in which respectful interaction brings the talents of all parties to bear on a problem.

There are three common models of working together: the *input* model, the *parallel* model, and the *collaborative* model. For our purposes, only the last model involves true collaboration. And, only the last model yields all the benefits of real collaboration.

In the *input* model, one team member creates a work product and the other team member responds to that work product. This is the approach used when a brief or contract is prepared by one team member alone and is then submitted to the other team member for review. Undeniably, there is some benefit to having the document reviewed by another. However, it yields only some of the benefits of true collaboration.

In the *parallel* model, one team member completes one set of tasks while another team member completes other tasks. One team member researches one set of issues while the other team member researches another set of issues. Again, there are benefits to this approach since work may be parceled out among many. However, the parallel model likewise yields only some of the benefits of true collaboration.

In the true *collaborative* model both team members participate in every phase from brainstorming through implementation. This does not mean that both team members perform every representational task together. It does mean that before a letter is written by one team member, both team members discuss the goals of the letter and the strategy to be employed to achieve those goals. Team members will also discuss any significant issues that must be addressed in the letter.

Similarly, in conducting a fact investigation plan, both team members do not have to be present when every witness is interviewed. However, both team members must participate in developing the fact investigation plan. And, both team members need to discuss the goals for each witness interview and the strategy to be employed in each such interview.

By undertaking true collaboration, the insights and viewpoints of each team member can be brought to bear. Each work product is strengthened by the participation of the entire team in developing the plan for completing that task and in identifying the choices inherent in that plan and the strategies to be employed in making those choices. Through effective collaboration, maximum use can be made of the experiences and knowledge that each collaborator brings to the joint work.

E. Characteristics of Effective Collaboration

Since collaboration is not automatically the result of working "together" with another person, it is important to understand the characteristics of effective collaboration if one is to realize its benefits. And, no characteristic is as important as is a healthy respect for differences in opinion between team members.

Collaboration is a process that cherishes differences and recognizes the benefits of constructive conflict. Conflict is not only inevitable, it is valued in collaboration because it brings to the table the differences in insights, life experiences, and sometimes values, of team members. The real question is how that conflict plays out in practice. In order to be "constructive," conflict must be undertaken with respect for the views of others and with a willingness to fight fairly. Winning at all costs cannot be an operative principle if effective collaboration is going to take place.

Closely related to constructive conflict is the decisionmaking process used in true collaboration. Collaboration embraces a process that structures joint decisionmaking in a non-hierarchical fashion. Team members must treat each other as equals and all must participate equally in the decisionmaking process. That, however, does not mean that respect is not paid to the views of a team member who may have special expertise as it relates to a particular issue. What it does mean is that team members do not have special status because of gender, race, age or other factors unrelated to the specific issues under consideration.

Finally, as in many longstanding relationships, humor, especially self-deprecating humor, and honesty play important roles in facilitating collaboration. The ability to laugh at one's self (and sometimes at/with one's partner) without malice or self-consciousness is a critical ingredient. And, the honest presentation and acceptance of views is critical to effective collaboration over the long run.

F.   Selecting Partners

In those clinics in which students work in teams, there are two approaches to pairing students: pairing by professor and pairing by students. If you have the option of selecting your own partner, think carefully before making your choice. You will spend a lot of time with that person and a successful partnership can add greatly to the clinical experience.

Ordinarily, it is *not* wise to pick a close friend or a roommate as a partner. While that may seem counter-intuitive, there are at least three reasons for this. First, you will have already developed patterns to your communications and roles in your relationships that may be very different from the patterns and roles of successful collaborators. Second, you may be able to bring greater diversity (of gender or race or age or life experiences) to your partnership by picking a different student as your partner. Third, if the partnership is not completely successful, you will not want to also risk a friendship in the process.

If you are being paired by your professor, you may wonder about the reasons for his/her pairing decisions. While diversity is often a primary factor in pairing decisions, there are other factors that may play a role. One team member may be better in oral communication while the other team member is better in written advocacy. One team member may be stronger at legal research while the other team member is better in fact investigation. Even such mundane factors as overlap in work hours and team access to a motor vehicle can play a role in the decisionmaking process. Professors try to gain as much information as they can about students early in the clinical experience to make these decisions.

G.   Collaboration and Clinic

Whatever the model in your clinic, try on the collaborative model in the same way you are experimenting with other forms of clinical methodology. Clinic is a wonderful opportunity to experiment and to test the various models of lawyering presented in clinic. And, remember to share your experiences and insights with regard to collaboration as you discuss your other experiences and insights in case supervision and in other settings.

While you are trying on the collaborative model, remember that collaboration is hardly the strong suit of many lawyers and even of many teachers. Much teaching is done alone and many lawyers refuse to relinquish power necessary to engage in effective collaboration. Even the media depictions of attorney collaboration are not always positive. In the coverage of the O.J. Simpson trial, for example, many cartoons highlighted the visible hostility between the members of the Simpson defense team.

While there is obviously much that is accurate in this depiction, there is also much that this depiction misses. The depiction fails to capture the connection with the jury that Johnnie Cochran brought to the defense, the expertise in DNA that Barry Scheck brought to the team, the cross-examination skills that F. Lee Bailey brought to the representation, and the connection to the Los Angeles media that Robert Shapiro brought to the trial strategy. And, their success in defending O.J. Simpson in the criminal case is a graphic reminder of the ways that "the whole" of a legal team can be greater than the sum of its parts. So, give collaboration a chance, but don't be afraid to critique it and your efforts at collaboration as you reflect on your clinical experience.

Chapter 10

Fact Investigation

It is the first day of your Contracts class in your first year of law school. The professor enters the room and, after arranging her/his teaching materials, s/he addresses the student next to you. The following dialogue takes place.

"Mr./Ms. Jones. Can you tell us the facts of *Sherwood v. Walker*?"

"Well, the defendant, Mr. Walker, sold this cow, Rose 2d of Aberlone, to the plaintiff, Mr. Sherwood. Both parties believed that the cow was barren. However, when the defendant discovered that the cow was pregnant and therefore worth more than the contract price, he tried to get out of the contract."

Even if your first class in law school did not discuss Rose 2d of Aberlone, the dialogue above is probably still pretty close to what you did experience in that first class. "What are the facts of . . ." are the first words of many law professors initiating a Socratic dialogue with their students, regardless of the subject matter of the course. But, *are those the facts?*

Throughout law school, you have dealt with packaged facts. In reading appellate cases, you have processed "facts" assembled by the judge writing the opinion for the court. Often, those "facts" were chosen by the appellate judge to support his/her opinion. You have sometimes had to deal with different "facts," as in *Sherwood v. Walker*, assembled by a dissenting judge. Again, however, those "facts" were packaged by the dissenting judge to support his/her opinion. In your examinations, you have worked with facts packaged by your professors in hypothetical problems to which you had to apply legal principles.

In real life, however, facts do not come "packaged." They must be developed by lawyers to tell stories on behalf of their clients. Often, these stories differ in the points they emphasize and sometimes these stories are mutually inconsistent. Moreover, although we refer to "facts" as if they were fully determinable, we will discover that ordinarily we will never know what the actual "facts" are, only what we believe to be true or what the evidence appears to demonstrate. Lawyers must also give these facts meaning by placing them in a context or contexts defined by the problems identified by the clients and by relating them to a solution or solutions designed to achieve some or all of our clients' goals.

Our roles in these circumstances are as "finder of facts" and "teller of stories." As "finder of facts," we will need to do things that law school has not required us to do previously—to develop a fact investigation plan and then to implement this plan. And, as "teller of stories," we will need to craft these facts into compelling stories to persuade judges, juries and other audiences to take actions that will further our clients' interests.

A.   The Importance of Fact Investigation

In the 1970s, Frances Kahn Zemans and Victor G. Rosenblum surveyed the Chicago bar for the American Bar Foundation study on "the making of a public profession." The study was conducted to identify the skills most important to the practice of law and the extent to which law schools provided law students with training in those skills. Through such a study, the authors hoped to identify the level of consonance or dissonance between legal education and the practice of law.

It is no great surprise that the authors concluded that legal education did not do a very good job of providing law students with the skills that they would need as lawyers. And, in probably no area was this dissonance more obvious than with regard to the skill of fact gathering (or fact investigation in our model).

The following chart describes the relative importance of some of the various lawyering skills as evaluated by Zemans and Rosenblum:

Skill/area of knowledge	Importance score	% rating important	% extremely important
Fact gathering	**72**	**93.0**	**69.7**
Substantive knowledge	66	90.1	42.3
Legal research	64	80.6	44.5
Negotiating	63	78.9	44.0
Drafting	61	74.2	40.8
Interviewing	51	58.1	22.8

These lawyers gave "fact gathering" an importance score of 72—the highest of any lawyering skill (or area of knowledge). Ninety-three percent of these lawyers evaluated "fact gathering" as an "important" lawyering skill and nearly 70 percent of these lawyers evaluated "fact gathering" as an "extremely important" lawyering skill—by far the highest ranking.

As indicated in the following table, when recent graduates were surveyed, only 16 percent stated that they had learned "fact gathering" in law school. And yet, 31 percent of the lawyers surveyed, nearly twice the number of law graduates who claimed to have developed this skill, expected law students to bring this skill to practice after graduation.

Skill/area of knowledge	% who learned in law school	% expected to bring skill/area
Fact gathering	**16**	**31**
Substantive knowledge	79	78
Legal research	75	91
Negotiating	2	3
Drafting	11	31
Interviewing	2	8

Although subsequent studies have reached somewhat different results on the relative importance of particular skills, fact gathering continues to be evaluated as a critical skill for practicing attorneys. Why is fact gathering rated so highly by practicing lawyers? And, why is there such a disparity between the importance of fact investigation and the ability of recent graduates to practice this skill after graduation from law school? The answers to these questions tell us a great deal about the focus of clinical legal education.

B.   What Do We Mean by Fact Investigation?

The term "fact investigation" encompasses two methods for obtaining information related to a client's circumstances—informal discovery and formal discovery. Formal discovery includes those methods authorized by or mandated by rules of civil or criminal procedure or by federal or state constitutions. In the context of civil proceedings, these methods include interrogatories, depositions, requests for production of documents, requests for physical or mental examination, and requests for admissions. In the context of criminal proceedings, these methods include constitutionally-required disclosure by prosecutors of exculpatory information and sharing of witness lists, statements, and alibi defenses required by rules of criminal procedure and federal and state constitutions.

One of the obvious limiting factors in factual investigation pursuant to formal discovery is that, with minor exceptions, formal discovery depends on the pendency of a civil or criminal action. That means that obtaining facts to determine whether a civil action should be filed or to persuade prosecutors to decline to initiate a prosecution must ordinarily depend on informal discovery techniques.

Informal discovery includes the range of investigative methods that do not depend on legal procedures. Interviews with witnesses, research into public records, photographs of accident or crime scenes, and research into news reports are among the forms of factual investigation included within informal discovery. We tend to focus on formal discovery in traditional law school classes like civil and criminal procedure, but informal discovery may have numerous advantages over formal discovery. Although we will discuss comparative benefits of informal and formal discovery later in this chapter, one potential advantage of informal discovery is that opposing counsel will not automatically be put on notice by your efforts as it will when formal discovery is invoked.

C. Role of Fact Investigation

As we discussed in chapter 5, our various client theories depend on the telling of persuasive stories to a number of different audiences. In the context of legal advocacy on behalf of our clients, we referred to these "stories" as the factual theory component of case theory. This factual theory part of case theory is a story presented through witnesses and exhibits.

Fact investigation provides us with the witnesses and exhibits we need to tell our stories. Through our fact investigation plan, we will develop a pool of potential witnesses and exhibits—the raw sources for telling client stories. Without effective fact investigation, we would therefore not have the building blocks for our storytelling. There would be stories to tell, but no way to tell them. That is why fact investigation is such an important focus of lawyering and of clinical legal education.

D. Telling Persuasive Stories

The goal of our factual theories is to persuade our audiences (often a judge or jury, but sometimes an opponent or opposing counsel) that our client's version of the facts is closer to the "truth" than is the version advanced by our adversaries. By getting our audience to acknowledge the "truth" of our story, we hope to persuade our audience to take an action favorable to our client or to withhold an action unfavorable to our client. Through this persuasion we will thereby further the realization of our client's goals. And, as this cartoon reminds us, the objective facts may neither be determinable nor accepted as such by our audiences.

But, what facts are important in this storytelling effort? If we are defending a client charged with arson, isn't the only relevant fact whether or not our client set the fire? If we are suing on behalf of a plaintiff injured in an automobile accident, isn't the only relevant fact whether our client was injured through the defendant's negligence?

There are several answers to the question of what facts are relevant. First, our client theory defines the scope of the relevant facts. If our client theory in a defense to a charge of arson depends on diminished capacity, facts beyond causation of the fire will be critical to that client theory. For example, we will need to present evidence regarding our client's mental state before and after the fire as well as expert testimony regarding mental status.

Second, if we think about the stories that have stayed with us over time, about the stories that have been most persuasive, these stories do not focus solely on a single critical event or a single moment in time—a murder, an accident, an incident of domestic violence. Instead, they ordinarily represent a detailed, chronological narration of interrelated events with a beginning point, connecting points, and a termination point—with events that occurred both before and after the "focus event." And so, our fairy tales begin with the language, "Once upon a time . . . ." The protagonists are then introduced, "And then a dragon terrorized the townspeople . . . , but a hero emerged from the crowd . . . ." The "focus event" is then described, "A ferocious battle ensued and the hero finally slew the dragon . . . ." And the story then concludes with the language, "And the people lived happily ever after." The critical event, the slaying of the dragon, is only a part of a much larger (and more persuasive) story.

Third, audiences normally want to hear not just what happened, but why things happened as we claim they did. They may find a defendant guilty of a crime, but they will want to know why the defendant committed the crime; they may find for a petitioner in a case seeking a civil protection order; but they will want to know why the respondent behaved as s/he did. A good story therefore normally focuses on substantively critical events, but it also surrounds those events with details of behaviors and happenings that came before and after.

E.   The Importance of a Good Story

We come through law school conditioned by our reading of appellate cases. As we have discussed, facts are abstracted and packaged in these opinions. And, because the focus of our analysis is generally on distilling the principles of law underlying these decisions, the importance of facts—of storytelling—often takes a back seat to legal analysis.

In real life, however, most cases are won or lost on the facts. In a custody matter, the parties are not in disagreement about the legal principle to be applied; the parties agree that the court must determine what custody arrangement is in the best interests of the children involved. The real question is a factual one: What custody arrangement is in the best interests of the children? And, the determination of that question requires a factfinder to sort through competing factual theories or stories.

Similarly, in a tort case, there will ordinarily be no dispute as to the applicable law. Both parties agree that negligence principles apply to the determination of fault, causation, and damages. The real questions are factual ones: Who was at fault and to what degree? To what extent did that fault cause the accident? And, what damages were the product of that negligent behavior? Again the issues of liability will be determined on the basis of whose story is more persuasive, not on the law applicable to the incident.

The client story or factual theory is the vehicle through which we attempt to persuade an audience to want to help our client, to provide our client with the relief or remedy we are seeking. In this formulation, the law (or legal theory) is seldom more than a "peg" on which the factfinder can hang a decision providing us with that relief or remedy. We therefore now turn to the factors that make stories persuasive to factfinders.

F. Factors Affecting Persuasiveness of a Story

1. Internal Consistency

A good story is internally consistent. Each piece of the story fits with the next and the elements of the story make sense as a whole. That does not mean that an individual who behaves cowardly in one section of the story cannot behave as a hero in another part of the story. However, that apparent internal inconsistency must be explained to the satisfaction of the audience or the credibility of the entire story will be undercut.

2. External Consistency

Is the story consistent with established facts? A story that depends on a snowstorm in Washington, D.C. in the summertime runs contrary to common experience. A lawyer must be prepared to establish the facts of that freak snowstorm.

Is the story consistent with prior tellings? One of the favorite techniques for impeachment is to get an adverse witness to tell a story again and again. Each time a narrator tells a story there are likely to be differences— some significant and some insignificant. However, each inconsistency will be exploited as a way of undercutting the credibility of the entire story.

3. Explanation

A good story should explain not only what happened, but it should explain why things happened as we claim they did. When someone is claimed to have taken an action, factfinders usually want to understand why the individual would have taken that action. That is why motive is ordinarily so important an element of criminal prosecutions.

4. Adequacy of Detail

Does the story contain sufficient (but not too many) details to make it credible? Stories can overwhelm with minutia and thereby lose an audience. However, stories devoid of detail are not realistic and do not usually resonate well with an audience. Audiences like to be able to picture individuals and events from a story. Detail is necessary to help paint that picture for the audience.

5.   Emotional Content

Does the story make the trier of fact sympathetic to the party? Human nature makes it more likely for a factfinder to decide in favor of a party with whom s/he has sympathy. Unlikeable parties often suffer disproportionately in the resolution of disputes—either through findings of liability or through assessment of damages. We even have a name for this factor—the victim discount. In a criminal proceeding, a defendant is likely to get a lighter sentence if the victim is unsympathetic; in a civil proceeding, a plaintiff is likely to be awarded lesser damages if s/he is unsympathetic.

6.   Socio-Political Content

Is the story consistent with socio-political attitudes and opinions of the factfinder? Although we may be aware of the impact of socio-political attitudes and opinions on major cases—the impact of a racist judge on a civil rights case, for example—socio-political attitudes and opinions can affect small cases as well. Evictions, divorces, and misdemeanor trials can all be influenced by the attitudes and opinions of factfinders. As noted in chapter 5, we need to identify these attitudes and opinions and then we need to address them through such basic approaches as the way the client is "packaged" for trial.

G.   A Caution in Thinking About Factual Theory

In applying these factors to develop a persuasive story, remember that persuasiveness can only be judged in relation to an audience. Lawyers sometimes develop stories that they think are persuasive and forget the differences in perception between themselves and judges, juries, and others. So, consciously work to not become a prisoner to your own experience. This is similar to the problem of attorney gap-filling. At trial (and in other settings), it is the factfinder's experience, not the attorney's, which determines the persuasiveness of a factual theory. A story that would be persuasive to one judge might not be persuasive to the judge in this cartoon. We therefore need to learn as much as we possibly can about our intended audience in order to tailor our stories to that audience's perceptions.

"What are you—some kind of justice freak?"

H. Factors Affecting Plausibility of a Witness

The factors affecting plausibility of a witness are similar to the factors affecting plausibility of stories. Since stories are largely told through witnesses, this should not come as any great surprise to us. Let us therefore now examine the factors that affect the plausibility of witnesses.

1. Competency

Is the witness competent in the area of his/her testimony? For an expert, this may seem obvious. The expert must have educational background and/or professional experience in the areas of his/her testimony. However, competency is also an issue for lay witnesses. Lay witnesses providing eyewitness testimony must have had the physical ability to see the events and the mental ability to process those observations.

2. Motive

Is the witness motivated by bias, interest or other motive concerning the subject matter of his/her testimony? One of the first questions posed to expert witnesses in cross-examination is the amount of their compensation for testimony. Factfinders tend to be naturally suspicious of witnesses whose testimony is "bought." However, motive can arise in many other forms. Does the witness have a longstanding antipathy to a party? Does the witness have a track record regarding the subject matter of his/her testimony? Fact investigation needs to be undertaken to identify underlying motives to strengthen favorable witnesses and to weaken adverse witnesses.

3.   Status

Does the witness have a status to which we ordinarily extend credibility? Probably the classic witness to whom we accord special status is a nun. However, many other witnesses bring with them status baggage that either elevates or detracts from their credibility as witnesses.

As captured in this cartoon, who would be a better (a more credible) expert witness than "Smokey the Bear" in a case involving a forest fire? By contrast, in a criminal prosecution against defendants allegedly engaged in organized crime, we may be forced to rely on witnesses with long criminal records who have accepted plea bargains and who may have even been placed in witness protection programs. The important thing is to recognize the role that status (and motive) may play in factfinder assessment of witness credibility and to address that issue squarely in our trial preparation. Like many other credibility factors, status is not a fixed value, but one that can be manipulated to achieve client goals through appropriate planning and implementation.

4.   Physical and Demographic Characteristics

Do the physical appearance, personal background, and other characteristics of the witness add to or detract from the way the factfinder will perceive the witness? We all operate under certain stereotypes of what physical and demographic characteristics add to or detract from the credibility of witnesses. One of the prime stereotypes in our society is that of the "dumb blonde." However, stereotypes are by no means uniform throughout society. When we have a choice about which witnesses to call to prove a particular element of our case, we need to know which witnesses are likely to be perceived most favorably by what class of factfinders. That determination may require the use of a trial consultant and the use of mock juries.

I.   A Caution in Thinking About Witnesses/Evidence

Again, don't become a prisoner to your own experience. This is similar to the problem of evaluating persuasiveness of stories. At trial, it is the factfinder's experience, not the attorney's, which determines the persuasiveness of witnesses/evidence.

A further caution: do not limit yourself to thinking only about admissible evidence. At early stages in case preparation, it is impossible to know what witnesses may be called or what evidence will be admissible or even relevant to the case we may have to present. We therefore must cast a wide net at these stages and winnow down our potential witnesses and evidence if and when we move closer to trial. At early stages we will therefore remind ourselves constantly to think about all legally relevant evidence—evidence that proves or disproves any elements of our client theories, evidence that strengthens or weakens our client or any of our potential witnesses, and evidence that adds to or detracts from any of the stories that we might tell.

J.   Direct and Circumstantial Evidence

Some evidence texts distinguish between direct and circumstantial evidence. Direct evidence is evidence that proves or disproves, without the need for an inference, an element that a party must establish. The classic example of direct evidence cited in many texts is eyewitness testimony that an individual committed a crime. Circumstantial evidence is evidence that, if believed, permits one to infer the existence of another fact.

In their text on FACT INVESTIGATION, David Binder and Paul Bergman created two rules of evidence to debunk this distinction.

Rule No. 1 provided that, "All evidence is either direct or circumstantial." Rule No. 2 provided that, "There is no such thing as direct evidence."

Binder and Bergman were not simply being humorous in their presentation of these two rules. By creating these two rules they reminded us that *all* evidence requires some inferences. For example, the testimony that a witness saw the defendant shoot the victim requires inferences that the witness was in a position to see the incident, that the witness had the physical ability to see the incident, that the witness had the mental ability to process the information to identify the nature of the incident and the identities of the parties, that . . . . The list of inferences inherent in this purported direct evidence is almost endless.

Other commentators have described this distinction in somewhat different terms. In his treatise, Graham Lilly explained that, "When direct evidence of a consequential proposition is presented . . . the trier is concerned solely with whether to believe the witness." Lilly contrasted this role of the trier of fact in dealing with circumstantial evidence. "[W]hen circumstantial evidence is introduced . . . the trier not only must be concerned with whether to believe the witness, but also with whether the evidence increases the probability of the proposition to which it is directed . . . ."

The identification and testing of inferences is a critical part of the work of trial lawyers (and sometimes judges and juries). The classic stage play (and later, movie) "Twelve Angry Men" describes the efforts by some members of a jury to test out the inferences inherent in such purportedly "direct" testimony as that of an eyewitness who testified to having seen the defendant kill his father. As the play makes clear, "direct" testimony is often merely complex "circumstantial" evidence. And, the inferences underpinning that circumstantial evidence may be unsupportable.

K. Trial by Inference

Binder and Bergman also describe a model of "Trial by Inference" that lawyers often find extremely useful. They focus on the "generalizations" that link pieces of circumstantial evidence to the elements of the factual theory of the case. These generalizations may be derived from universal principles of physical science or from the general behavior of people or things. By linking these pieces of circumstantial evidence to their inferences, these generalizations allow a factfinder to infer (or to piggyback) from an item of evidence to a conclusion on the strength of a premise.

For example, in a criminal case in which a law student is charged with theft, the prosecutor might introduce evidence that the defendant was facing huge tuition bills. In the "Trial by Inference" model, the prosecutor is using a generalization—that people in financial crisis are likely to steal in order to obtain money. The circumstantial evidence (that the defendant is in need of money) is linked to the conclusion (that the defendant is the thief) by the generalization (that people who are in need of money are likely to steal in order to meet that need). The equation "Evidence + Generalization = Inference" captures this approach.

Binder and Bergman then urge lawyers to test out the strength or accuracy of generalizations by adding the words "except when" and "especially when" to allow us to analyze the probative value of evidence in terms of the strength of the generalizations. Generalizations vary in accuracy. They may be true almost always, usually true (more often than not), sometimes true (less often than 50%), or rarely true.

Investigators use these generalizations all the time in searching for facts. In her article "The Rightful Owner," Susan Sheehan described the efforts of an investigator, Edward Goldfader, to track down the heirs of a deceased shareholder. After researching the basic facts of the decedent's life, Goldfader observed that the decedent was Catholic and was born in the nineteenth century. He then put forward the generalization that Catholics born in the nineteenth century were seldom only children. Therefore, Goldfader hypothesized (inferred), the decedent probably had siblings. That hypothesis then suggested a particular line of factual investigation to identify the family tree through birth certificates and baptismal records. Similarly, the facts that the decedent bought stock in one company and was a lawyer and was in his 80s at the time of his death led Goldfader to the generalization that 80 year-old lawyers seldom buy stock in only one company. Therefore, Goldfader hypothesized (inferred) that the decedent probably owned stock in other corporations. That hypothesis then suggested a different line of factual investigation to check with other stock corporations to see if Goldfader owned additional shares and if he might have transferred any of those shares to family members.

L. Testing our Hypotheses

As Binder and Bergman suggest, we will use a three-step test as part of our factual investigation plan to test the strength of our generalizations and to find legally relevant evidence. In Step 1, we will articulate the generalization that links the "fact" to the factual hypothesis. In Step 2, we will add "except when" to the generalization to test its accuracy and to identify evidence to rebut the hypothesis. In Step 3, we will add "especially when" to identify evidence needed to buttress the hypothesis and to highlight the possible need to narrow the generalization in order to strengthen it.

In the theft example above, the generalization in Step 1 is that "Law students in need of money are likely to resort to theft." In Step 2, we would add the words "except when" to yield "Law students in need of money are likely to resort to theft except when . . . ." We might come up with the possibility that "Law students in need of money are likely to resort to theft except when they have wealthy relatives who will loan them money." In our fact investigation plan, we would investigate to see whether the defendant had such "wealthy relatives" and whether those relatives had loaned them money. Or we might come up with the possibility that "Law students in need of money are likely to resort to theft except when they have a scholarship or loan application pending." In our fact investigation plan, we would then investigate to see whether the defendant had potential sources of scholarships or loans.

Finally, in Step 3, we would add the words "especially when" to yield "Law students in need of money are likely to resort to theft especially when . . . ." We might come up with the possibility that "Law students in need of money are likely to resort to theft especially when their relatives are unwilling to assist them financially." In our fact investigation plan, we would investigate the financial abilities and temperaments of such relatives. Or we might come up with the possibility that "Law students in need of money are likely to resort to theft especially when they have exhausted all sources of scholarships or loans." In our fact investigation plan, we would then investigate to see whether the defendant had "maxed" out his/her financial assistance or was otherwise disqualified from such assistance.

M. Developing a Fact Investigation Plan

Although Perry Mason aficionados may vaguely remember Perry turning Paul Drake, his private investigator, loose with only the most general instructions, real lawyers need to begin their fact investigation with the development of a plan to guide their efforts and those of their agents. In developing this plan, lawyers need to answer a series of six questions: (1) What evidence should be obtained? (2) Where should that evidence be obtained? (3) How should that evidence be obtained? (4) What types of formal/informal discovery should you utilize? (5) By whom should that evidence be obtained? (6) When should that evidence be obtained? and, (7) How much evidence is enough? We will examine each of those questions in turn.

1.   What Evidence Should Be Obtained?

We will need evidence to establish each of the factual elements of each theory of the case. In order to identify this evidence, it is ordinarily helpful to create a matrix for each distinct client theory. In each matrix, we would then describe each theory in factual terms and break out each element of each factual theory. The matrix might look something like this:

Theory of the case: Our client's husband committed adultery. Although state law requires a period of non-cohabitation for a divorce, that waiting period does not apply if adultery can be proven. Therefore, our client can file for divorce without satisfying the one-year period of non-cohabitation.

Element: The husband had the disposition to commit adultery.

Evidence proving this element	Husband was arrested several times for solicitation of prostitutes.
Information undercutting this element	Husband was only convicted of disorderly conduct on two of these occasions.
Evidentiary concerns with this evidence	Are arrest (non-conviction) records admissible? Need to lay foundation for court files Need to subpoena police officers
Sources of information	Court records Police department files
Investigative method	Informal discovery—send investigator down to court to obtain complete court files Informal discovery—send investigator to interview police officers and try to secure copies of notes

As we discussed in chapter 5, in order for the factual theory to be legally sufficient, we will need to have evidence on each required element. If we do not have evidence to prove each element of our claim (or defense), our case will fail. This is the factual equivalent of a FRCP 12(b)(6) when a complaint fails to allege facts sufficient to state a claim for relief.

How will we figure out the elements of each factual theory that we will need to prove in order to prevail? In order to identify each of these "required" elements we will refer to statutes and regulations and to case law. However, we may also be able to shortcut our work, an important value in private law firms and in public interest practices, by using such tools as charging documents in criminal cases and pattern jury instructions in civil and criminal matters.

While litigation charts or fact investigation plans are useful tools for lawyers, there are certain disadvantages in relying on them too much. They are useful in helping us to identify what we need to prove or disprove, but they tend to narrow our inquiry to the elements of our potential claims and/or defenses at the expense of circumstantial and other forms of evidence. Fact investigation plans are also useful in pinpointing the strengths and weaknesses of our cases and those of our adversaries. However, these plans often focus our attention on "what evidence needs to be obtained" and "how that evidence needs to be obtained" at the expense of "when that evidence needs to be obtained" and "by whom that evidence should be obtained." So, while we will use such litigation charts, we will be conscious of their limitations in order to minimize the potential disadvantages while maximizing the benefits.

Once we decide on the kinds of evidence that need to be obtained, we will need to focus on the forms of evidence that should be obtained. Evidence can be obtained in the form of oral testimony, written testimony, or documentary evidence. Oral testimony will rise or fall on the credibility of the witness. Written testimony may present hearsay and other objections. Documentary evidence may require a foundation and authentication. Like many aspects of litigation, there are no general rules to apply here in determining what kind of evidence is best, but ordinarily we will explore alternative types of evidence that can help us prove the elements of our case. Otherwise, all our eggs will be left in a single basket.

2.   Where Should that Evidence Be Obtained?

Evidence can be obtained from a variety of sources. It can be obtained from clients. Or, it can be obtained from persons with an "interest" in the outcome or in the proceedings themselves. It can be obtained from experts (technically a subclass of interested persons since they have a "financial interest" in the proceedings). Or, it can be obtained from disinterested persons (a fairly rare commodity). Finally, it can be obtained from adverse parties (and their representatives).

Evidence obtained from clients is ordinarily the cheapest and fastest way to secure evidence. However, it is also the most unreliable in the eyes of most audiences because of the self-interest of clients. Much of this can also be said of interested persons, although experts are an accepted form of interested persons in most legal proceedings. Despite this fact, factfinders often discount the value of expert testimony and testimony of other interested persons, especially since they are often confronted with dueling experts at trial.

There are steps that can be taken to increase the credibility of even the most self-interested witnesses. Who would ordinarily be less believable than a former mobster who has entered a federal witness protection program? The mobster has entered into an agreement with the government to provide particular testimony. The mobster comes with a "life in crime" pedigree that ordinarily is not the stamp of a credible witness. The mobster is getting compensation (an allowance) for his testimony. However, effective preparation of the witness for cross-examination or a direct examination that anticipates the potential weak credibility of the witness, can turn weakness into strength. So, anticipated problems in credibility of a witness are not necessarily fatal. Like many other aspects of lawyering, they are an issue that must be identified and addressed. By effectively anticipating and defusing the shortcomings in credibility, an otherwise unreliable witness can be made into a persuasive witness to tell a persuasive story.

Disinterested persons would appear to be the most reliable and accepted sources of evidence. However, one must critically examine the extent to which they are actually disinterested. Even if they do not appear to be interested in the outcome, they may be interested in the process—in being recognized for their ability to play a role in the determination of a dispute. Again, the texts of the play and screenplay in "Twelve Angry Men" provide an excellent example of a witness for whom the chance to testify represented a moment of limited stardom in a lifetime of largely being ignored.

3.   How Should that Evidence Be Obtained?

Should you utilize formal or informal discovery to obtain evidence? Formal discovery will put the opposing side on notice. How much do you want/need to keep your efforts secret? Evidence obtained from formal discovery is usually easier to introduce into evidence. How important to you is that consideration? Formal discovery brings the potential compulsion of the court along with it. How easy will it be for you to obtain the evidence without some form of compulsion? In the absence of court compulsion, are there facilitating factors that you can employ to get a witness to open up?

Informal discovery may be cheaper since you will not need to incur costs for court reporters or deposition transcripts. However, by incurring costs up front through formal discovery, will the long-term costs actually be lower? Informal discovery may be faster since you can begin the process immediately without being subject to timelines imposed by court rules. Will speed be a benefit or a detriment in your effort to obtain needed evidence? The non-intimidating aspects of informal discovery may make witnesses more willing to talk to you. But, if they change their story, will you be able to effectively impeach them?

4.   What Types of Formal/Informal Discovery Should You Utilize?

Even within a particular kind of discovery (formal or informal), there are always multiple ways of getting information. If you have to choose, is it better to use interrogatories (which are cheaper) or depositions (which are more flexible)? Even if you have the financial ability and the time to use multiple forms of discovery, will one sequence or another yield better results?

5.   By Whom Should that Evidence Be Obtained?

Evidence can be obtained by a client, by the attorney, or by an investigator. When there is a choice, who should obtain needed evidence?

If the attorney obtains such evidence as a witness statement, who can the attorney put on the stand to impeach the witness if s/he changes her/his story? However, if the attorney is not present when the witness statement is taken, will the investigator or client be able to fully follow-up in areas that the attorney would have probed further?

If the client obtains evidence, will a judge or jury discount that evidence because of the self-interest of the client? Is the client sufficiently sophisticated to be able to effectively obtain complex evidence or to obtain a comprehensive witness statement?

Will a witness be willing to talk to an attorney who may be of a very different racial or economic background or of a different gender from a critical witness? Might the witness be more willing to communicate with an investigator who looks and sounds more like the witness? Will an investigator be able to effectively "size up" the credibility of the individual as a witness at trial?

Does the investigator possess techniques and skills that may produce more and better evidence than could be obtained by a client or attorney? For example, investigators often know how to seed witness testimony through the phrasing of questions. It is one thing to ask, "Do you remember the color of the car?" It is quite another to ask, "Do you remember seeing Mr. Gillis driving a blue car?" Investigators are aware of such techniques as getting a witness to initial a statement that they will not sign—although the initials will authenticate the statement every bit as much as a signature. Investigators are also aware of such techniques as purposely making a few errors in a witness statement and then asking the witness to correct those errors so that the witness cannot later avoid the statement by claiming that s/he did not review it.

6. When Should that Evidence Be Obtained?

Although some commentators suggest that you can use informal discovery before filing suit or before a prosecution is initiated and you can then use formal discovery after the suit is filed or after the prosecution is initiated, that formulation is neither accurate nor helpful. Informal discovery does not necessarily end with the filing of an action and formal discovery can precede the filing of an action.

Since all necessary evidence cannot be obtained at the same time, it is often necessary to sequence investigative efforts as part of a fact investigation plan. Must other evidence be obtained first in order to make a particular factual inquiry effective? Is it possible a critical witness for your side may disappear or die? If so, you will want to memorialize that testimony prior to that disappearance or death.

Is the evidence critical for pretrial motions? If so, efforts to obtain that evidence will ordinarily receive priority within an investigation plan. Is the evidence critical for negotiations? If so, efforts to obtain that evidence will have to precede the date for projected negotiations.

Will the attempt to get the evidence put the opposing side on notice too soon? If the opposing side has not yet begun to think about their case theory, perhaps you don't want to force them to work through their theories until late in the discovery process. If you are concerned that keeping the opposing side in the dark longer works to your client's benefit, then you will place those investigative efforts later in your fact investigation plan. Will the attempt to get the evidence force the opposing side to work up the case in a way that they might not otherwise? Many lawyers are slobs in their work habits and procrastinate whenever possible. If you are facing such a lawyer, anything that forces opposing counsel to start working on his/her case will ordinarily work to your disadvantage.

7. How Much Evidence is Enough?

Time constraints may limit the amount of evidence you can obtain. Under a scheduling order you only have so much time to conduct discovery. Financial constraints may limit the amount of evidence you can obtain. No clients have an unlimited discovery budget. But, even if time and finances do not constrain your fact investigation (and legal research), at some point you need to say "enough is enough!" In deciding when you have reached "enough," remember the example of General McClellan during the Civil War! As commander of Union forces, McClellan was urged by President Lincoln to attack the Confederate forces. McClellan's consistent response was that he needed more soldiers, and then more artillery, and then more soldiers. The result was paralysis and, ultimately, the replacement of McClellan as a commander.

It is always possible to investigate one more fact or research one more case. However, one more fact or one more case will never eliminate all the anxiety and uncertainty that is part of the practice of law. At some point, you need to decide that you have done enough and move forward on the basis of what you have.

Chapter 11

Counseling

"What do you think I should do?"

"Well, if I were you . . . ."

How many times have you engaged in the fragments of conversation depicted above? Friends have probably come to you to talk about boy/girl-friends, about job possibilities, about living arrangements, and about the myriad other details of personal life. Probably, you have prided yourself on the advice you have given, even if that advice was not ultimately taken. And, sometimes, whether the advice was taken or rejected, you have lost friends after counseling them.

Whether the model of "If I were you" is a good model for counseling friends and others, we will discover that it works poorly as a model for legal counseling. Instead, in this chapter we will look at a very different model of counseling, one that we believe will provide you with a more effective and more satisfying approach for assisting clients. In this "client-centered" model of counseling, we will constantly be asking ourselves, "What assistance does *this* client need from me to help him/her make informed decisions regarding the options available to him/her." And, we will constantly be searching for the tools and techniques that will facilitate this process for the particular clients we are counseling at any moment as they work through options to address their particular problems and to achieve their particular goals.

A. Relinquishing Decisionmaking Authority

One of the most difficult aspects of counseling experienced by many law students (and lawyers) is the situation in which, despite the student attorney's best efforts, the client insists on picking the "wrong" option. Even students who pledge allegiance to a client-centered model of representation sometimes find themselves engaged in the following dialogue:

> *Student*: Okay. I've reviewed with you the various options that are available. Do you have any questions about any of them?

Client: No. I think I understand the choices.

Student: Well, what do you want to do?

Client: I want to go ahead with the third option. That seems to be the best one for me.

Student: (expressing a mixture of disappointment and frustration) Well, I obviously didn't do a good job of laying out the options for you. Let me try it again.

This process is then repeated as many times as necessary until the client "gets it right."

Why is it so difficult to relinquish decisionmaking to our clients? Certainly there are a variety of reasons. We feel a tremendous sense of responsibility to our clients, especially to our first clients in clinic. We are therefore reluctant to see these clients experience anything but the "best" outcomes. We also feel insecure about the fulfillment of our attorney responsibilities. Almost counter-intuitively, we then respond to this insecurity by wanting to take more control of the case. We may even be reluctant to share a client's decisions with our supervisor, fearing that somehow we may be held accountable for those choices.

All of these factors (and more) contribute to a reluctance to yield decisionmaking authority to our clients. As we will discover, this is a reluctance that we must fight to overcome.

B. Fuzzy Counseling

One of the reasons why clients make decisions against our "best" advice is that we fail to recognize the "fuzzy" nature of "option evaluation." Too often we evaluate options based on our own decision matrix, a matrix that weighs options based on our own criteria of value. When our clients apply a different decision matrix, we can't understand why they reach different conclusions.

In a criminal defense clinic, for example, a student attorney receives a plea bargain offer from the prosecuting attorney. Under the offer, the client must plead guilty to a lesser-included offense but will receive no jail time. When the student attorney ranks this option as a member of the fuzzy set of ideal choices, this option ranks at or nearly 1.0. It removes the risks associated with going to trial and the anxieties associated with facing those risks. Perhaps the student attorney also explicitly (albeit improperly) factors in her/his own needs—that s/he won't have to spend the weekend preparing for trial, that s/he won't run the risk of being embarrassed in court, that s/he won't have to face a judge that s/he is scared of.

By contrast, the client views the plea offer very differently. Her/his primary need may be an opportunity to tell her/his story in court—an interest that is necessarily compromised by a plea agreement. Although s/he certainly wants to avoid incarceration, that need is secondary to her/his need to have a "day in court." So, s/he rates the plea offer as a .6 member of the fuzzy set of ideal choices. Although the student attorney may initially perceive the client as making an uninformed choice, at least in the absence of a thorough identification of client goals and interests, the client is making a very informed choice, albeit one based on different values from those of the student.

We must therefore work hard to identify client goals and to evaluate each option as a member of the fuzzy set of options advancing or negating these goals. By comparing the level of membership for each alternative individually and in combination (for those options that are not mutually exclusive), the client can make an informed choice among and between the various fuzzy alternatives available.

In doing so, we will also be conscious of the need to make our presentation and weighing of options accessible to our clients. The use of terms like "fuzzy sets" and "degrees of membership" will probably be confusing for most clients. Our task is to develop language and a system of presentation that will actually work for the particular client we are counseling, even as we use the fuzzy thinking paradigm in the background for our purposes.

Being concrete and accessible in our presentation of options is sometimes sacrificed as we attempt to be non-directive in our client counseling. We can sometimes present advice and concerns in a way that can make them meaningless and inaccessible to our clients. So, we need to be conscious of the importance of keeping the client at the center of the decisionmaking process while not bending over so far backwards that we do not assist the client in that process.

C. Counseling Builds on Interviewing

In chapter 7, we observed that there is seldom a clear distinction between interviewing and counseling. In interviewing, we gathered facts, we built rapport and inspired confidence and we established an attorney-client relationship. In counseling, we *continue* to engage in all of those tasks. We *continue* to gather facts, we *continue* to build rapport and inspire confidence, and we *continue* to solidify our attorney-client relationship. However, counseling adds an additional "action" stage to this process. In counseling, we help our clients reach decisions. And, we should never lose sight of the outcome or product that counseling is undertaken to achieve—client decisions.

D. Helping the Client Reach a Decision

We should also remember that in a client-centered approach, it is the *client*, not the *lawyer*, who makes the decisions. Even though the ethical rules only require that clients make decisions about objectives of the representation and authorize lawyers to make decisions about the means by which those objectives are to be achieved (after consultation with clients), we will try to involve our clients to a far greater extent than the minimum ethical requirement. To the extent that our clients are able and willing, we will seek to involve our clients in all significant decisions regarding the scope and process of representation.

There are a variety of tools that effective counselors use to achieve these goals. In a very real sense, counseling builds on interviewing by utilizing all of the skills and values of effective interviewing—empathy, concreteness, genuineness, and respect. However, in counseling we will supplement these tools by adding structure, confrontation, and advice while also taking empathy to a higher (or more complex) level.

E. Structure

Presenting alternatives and then stepping back is not enough. If we are really going to help our clients decide which courses of action best meet their needs and priorities, we will need to do more than simply hint at problems and possible solutions. So, how will we go about actually making the counseling process work for our clients? The answer is found in providing counseling within a structure designed to help our clients assess information and reach decisions.

In interviewing, we discussed a series of stages—a structure—designed to achieve the various goals of the interviewing process. Counseling also ordinarily proceeds through a series of stages. However, whereas the ordering of stages in interviewing was not critical, counseling stages must necessarily proceed in a more linear manner.

1. Preparation

A good structure begins with effective preparation. It is possible to conduct an outstanding interview with little or no pre-knowledge of the facts or law relating to a client's concerns. However, it is impossible to effectively counsel a client without a complete grasp of the facts and law you began learning in the initial interview, expanded through your follow-up meetings with your client, and refined through your fact investigation and legal research. You need to understand the law and the facts so well that you can make that information accessible to your client. You will not be able to "wing" an effective counseling session if your client is going to make informed decisions.

You will also need to prepare to understand your client's goals. Throughout your clinical experience you have probably asked yourself (and probably your clinical supervisor), "What should I do here?" And the response was (or at least should have been), "Well, what are you trying to achieve?" None of our action steps are taken in a vacuum; they are all taken with regard to achieving a particular goal or set of goals. As this "Doonesbury" cartoon demonstrates, it is only in relation to goals that we can evaluate the wisdom of various options.

DOONESBURY © G.B. Trudeau. Reprinted with permission of UNIVERSAL PRESS SYNDICATE. All rights reserved.

Keeping in mind the relationship between goals and counseling is critical. All of our work so far has been designed to help clients identify their goals and to help plan and implement ways of achieving those goals. Without a clear understanding of our client's goals, we cannot effectively design or meaningfully evaluate options. And, as we will discover in looking at stages in the actual counseling session, we will need to clarify whether the goals our client articulated at the beginning of the lawyer-client relationship remain our client's goals these days (or weeks) later. We will therefore need to design a counseling model that is flexible and that can adapt to changes in client goals.

In addition to researching the law and investigating the facts in advance of the counseling session, we will need to determine how to make that information accessible to our clients. We will need to prepare language and approaches that will allow us to explain our investigative findings to our clients; we will also need to prepare language and approaches that will allow us to explain our conclusions regarding the possible interpretations of the law to our clients.

We will also need to clarify our goals for the counseling session. It may not be possible to review every option effectively with our clients at a single counseling session. Clients and lawyers only have limited energy and attention spans; it is possible to rapidly reach a point of diminishing returns in which the presenting of more options results in the less effective processing of any options. We will therefore need to start by identifying those options that must be presented and acted upon by our clients or they will be forever lost—either because they will be barred by a statute of limitations or because they will be preempted by other events.

Beyond the identification of those options that *must* be presented, we will need to decide how many options can effectively be presented and processed by our clients. What counseling goals can realistically be accomplished beyond the minimum set of goals that must be achieved?

Once we have completed this triage process, we will need to decide how to present alternatives to our clients. We will need to be sure to include both legal and non-legal (not illegal) avenues that address one or more aspects of our client's goals. We will need to identify the positive and negative consequences of each alternative. We will also need to evaluate the likelihood of success of each such alternative.

In discussing the likelihood of success of a particular option, we will need to keep a number of considerations in mind. We will need to develop a language of prediction that is concrete. Throughout law school we learned how to use "weasel" words to hedge our bets. After all, if we didn't take a position, we could hardly be held accountable for that position. We learned to use "weasel" words like "might probably" and "I definitely think you could." However, this type of language will deprive our clients of the concrete information they need to make informed decisions.

We also need to be aware of two contrary tendencies. The first is to unduly reassure our clients about the merits of their cases. We want our clients to like us and we want to give them good news. However, an unrealistically positive assessment of their cases may lead them to reject settlement offers that reflect the true value of their cases. Second, we must not understate the value of our clients' cases to assure success and satisfaction. All of us want our clients to think that we are heroes and terrific lawyers. If we give our clients unrealistically low values of their cases and then win much for them, they will naturally think that we are wonderful. However, by "low-balling" the value of a client's case, a client may accept a settlement offer that is far less than the true value of her/his case.

We will also need to determine in what order alternatives should be presented—the basic format of the counseling session. Such principles as "primacy and recency" (that we tend to remember and place importance on what we heard first and what we heard last) may lead our clients to place unintended significance on the order in which we present options. Even if disavow such significance in our discussions with our clients, they may impose significance on our ordering of options.

Finally, we will need to think about the extent to which visual aids may help our clients better process the information we are presenting to them. While lawyers sometimes use computer graphics and professional charts to achieve this purpose, far simpler and less costly models can be of benefit to clients in reaching informed decisions. For example, a lawyer might draw up the following table in advance of the counseling session with only the column headings filled out:

Option	Benefits	Disadvantages	Likelihood of success	Client reaction
1.				
2.				
3.				

In a counseling session, we can then complete this form with our client as we talk through each option and place a "√" or "X" or "?" as our client reacts to each option. Our client can also keep a copy of this completed grid and use it as a way of keeping track of the choices and plans for the steps ahead. Entries recording the "Client Reaction" also emphasize the central role of the client in the counseling process.

2.   Ice-Breaking

Counseling sessions ordinarily begin with some level of small talk or ice-breaking. It has probably been at least a few days since you last saw your client; it may be helpful to reestablish a connection with the client. The client may be anxious and a little small talk may help the client relax. At the same time, like most of our "rules," we will not apply this mechanically. Some clients may come in to a counseling session with an overriding need to learn what we have come up with as options. Any initial ice-breaking may then seem like a waste of time and add to the anxiety of the client.

One of the classic revelations that students experience when they watch themselves counsel clients in simulation exercises is that they, as the lawyer, talk almost all the time. They may even comment after the simulation that the client seemed disinterested or passive. However, the reality may be that the lawyer created a structure and defined a role for the client that effectively, if not intentionally, disempowered and marginalized the role of the client. Effective ice-breaking can create a conversational rhythm that will carry over to the presentation and discussion of options and thereby increase the role of the client in this process.

3.   Fact Updating

Facts are not static; they are dynamic. The client's life did not go into suspended animation after our initial (or even most recent) interview. Important events may have occurred. And, our counseling efforts must acknowledge that possibility and plan for it. At an early stage in the counseling process, we will therefore need to update with our clients the facts of their lives, especially the facts most relevant to the issues for which the clients sought legal assistance.

The client who sought help in filing for bankruptcy because of overwhelming bills may have been driven to seek legal assistance by harassing telephone calls by creditors. We need to know whether those creditors are continuing to call. The client who sought help in establishing a community organization to develop a child care center may have been driven to seek legal help because of the threatened closure of the only child care center in the area. We need to know whether that center is actually going to close, whether additional rental properties appropriate for the center may have opened in the community, and whether relationships among the various principals in the planned community corporate entity remain viable.

We can try to develop this information through directed questions about what we perceive as the most relevant facts. However, through such an approach we are likely to get only the facts we expect. As in interviewing, that is the great danger of relying too heavily on directed questions.

We can also use open-ended questions to get this information. Although something more than "So, what's new?" will probably be necessary to elicit useful information, open-ended questions have the potential to get us the facts that we do not expect, the facts that will often be most critical for us to factor into our counseling process.

For this reason, it is often helpful to blend ice-breaking with fact-updating. In the process of ice-breaking with the client, we can elicit updated facts about the client and his/her life. Through this approach we can then adapt our counseling plan in light of the inevitable factual developments to which we must respond.

4.   Goal Clarification

Like facts, client goals are not static. Intervening events may alter client goals or their priority—the fact that bill collectors stop calling takes the sense of urgency out of the option of seeking a restraining order to stop harassment. Client wishes may change—a client may think better (or at least differently) about how to resolve the potential conflict between competing goals. It is therefore essential that we make sure that we are counseling the actual client before us today and not a "constructed" client or the client who appeared before us in the initial interview or at some other interaction.

5.   Presentation and Review of Options

In our discussion of preparation, we discussed some of the issues related to the presentation and review of options with our clients. However, there are many other issues to consider.

The overriding issue relates to the role of the lawyer in the counseling process. In discussing fact investigation, we described the lawyer as "finder" (of facts) and "teller" (of stories). In the counseling process, we need to consciously struggle against the vision of lawyer as "knower and director." Many of us have been led to view lawyers as possessors of wisdom ("knowers") and directors of choices for our clients ("directors"). While there is certainly knowledge we have and information to share, we need to learn how to learn about our clients and their worlds and to find information and identify approaches to address our clients' problems. Otherwise, the vision of ourselves as simply "knower and director" will lead us to talk too much with inadequate knowledge of our clients and their lives and to direct solutions that seldom meet our client's needs.

Another important issue relates to the way that our clients should listen to the presentation of options. It may seem counter-intuitive, but clients generally do not know how to listen to the presentation of options. Can they choose only one option? If so, they will listen in a very different way to the presentation of options than if they can choose multiple options. In the former scenario, they will tend to remember only one option at a time; in the latter scenario, they will attempt to remember multiple complimentary or unrelated options. Helping the client understand the ground rules of how they should listen to the presentation of options can therefore yield important dividends.

From our earlier meetings with a client, we may have identified inconsistencies in client goals or an apparent failure of the client to confront specific issues. While there may be a variety of reasons why we did not address these inconsistencies or failures previously (perhaps we delayed confronting our client in order to focus on building rapport and client confidence), we would not be serving our client well if we left these concerns unaddressed in the counseling process.

However, we also need to figure out how to raise these concerns in an effective manner, while maintaining and furthering the attorney-client relationship. The process of raising these concerns is known as "probing" or "confrontation." However, whereas the term "confrontation" may suggest a full frontal assault on our client, the actual process of "probing" or "confrontation" involves a far more complex and subtle skill.

We might raise these concerns by presenting them in tentative language ("I wonder if these two goals—of maximizing your child support and alimony while maintaining a good relationship with your ex-spouse—might be inconsistent. What do you think?"). Such an approach gives the client the space to confront within her/himself the apparent inconsistency and either demonstrate why the goals are not inconsistent or recognize that inconsistency without feeling that s/he has been put on the defensive.

We might also ask the client to project the consequences of particular alternatives, giving the client the ability to identify for the "team" of lawyer and client the problems inherent in pursuing both approaches. We can also help the client by having her/him discuss feelings and priorities before presenting alternatives. In this way, we can avoid locking the client into a particular choice or set of choices from which the client will have to retreat.

One of the other ways that we can help the client address perceived inconsistencies is by providing space for the client to identify and cure informational gaps and ambiguities. Often a perceived inconsistency is simply the result of a failure on our part to fully understand the client's goals or a failure on our part to adequately explain the consequences of particular alternatives. Once the lawyer and client are fully informed, the result may either be a vanishing of the apparent inconsistency or a different set of choices by the client.

6. Decisionmaking

Ultimately, counseling is a stage in the lawyer-client relationship during which the client must make certain decisions. One of the potential weaknesses of the client-centered model is that it is sometimes ineffective in getting clients to make choices. It excels in establishing an atmosphere for the identification and discussion of choices, but it is not always as effective in helping the client to "pull the trigger." We need to be conscious of this tendency, but also not to create unnecessary time pressures. If an option will be waived by inaction, we need to identify that consequence—that the failure to act will be an action by default. However, if there are no external time pressures, the failure by the client to decide on a course of action to meet an artificial deadline may actually harm the client. When clients are given too many choices with too tight a time frame for decision, the client may simply freeze or choose the first or last option presented.

Delays in client decisionmaking may also demonstrate another inconsistency or complexity in the client's needs and goals that will have to be addressed by lawyer and client. For example, the client who repeatedly postpones signing a complaint for divorce once such requirements as physical separation have been satisfied may simply be demonstrating that s/he is not quite prepared to end her/his marriage. We may need to probe this issue through such tentative language as "I know that you authorized me to draft a complaint for divorce, but you have postponed coming in to sign the complaint several times. I wonder if you are not quite prepared to end your marriage." Sometimes making explicit what the client has seemed to demonstrate implicitly through action or inaction can help the client confront her/his true feelings.

Like many other lawyering techniques, confrontation has both benefits and risks. It is intended to enhance client self-exploration and self-understanding. But, in confronting the client with perceived inconsistencies, it forces the client to explain the conflict between information, values, statements, beliefs, or relationships. It therefore puts the client on the spot.

Such an approach can help spur a client to action, but it also forces a client to make a decision by confronting the client with the mutual exclusivity between achieving goals and remaining inactive. It can help ensure accuracy of lawyer understanding. It can also help clarify and correct conflicts in information and signals. But, it can strain the attorney-client relationship at a time when rapport and confidence are especially important.

Ineffective counselors avoid confrontation entirely or confine its use to non-threatening and neutral topics. Or, they may err on the other side and confront the client in an aggressive, attacking manner. So, while confrontation is a necessary tool for effective representation, it should ordinarily be avoided in the early stages of the lawyer-client relationship. Moreover, its use must be consistent with caring, empathic, respectful and genuine counseling. And, lawyers need to be aware that effective confrontation may require recognition of and adaptation to gender, race, and similar concerns.

7. Closure

In the final stage of the counseling process, the lawyer and client will recapitulate the decisions that have been made and identify the specific actions that will be taken and by whom the actions will be taken. Lawyer and client will also identify the intended timetable for taking those actions. Often, a new, superseding retainer will be executed to reflect the specific responsibilities that the lawyer has agreed to perform for the client and the arrangements as to court costs or other fees that the client may have agreed to assume. It is a moment for shared expectations in the future of the lawyer-client relationship.

F. Self-Disclosure

Another technique that can help a client work through complex decisions is counselor self-disclosure. Counselor self-disclosure can help demonstrate the nature and depth of the disclosure expected from your clients. It can also reduce the level of control and professional superiority by the lawyer over the client. Self-disclosure can help establish or cement a common bond between yourself and your clients. It can also provide valuable information to the client and can help clients better understand and analyze their own situations.

However, counselor self-disclosure can have several downsides. It can make you seem self-centered by shifting the focus from the client to you. It can also come across as patronizing. Since counselor self-disclosure relates to past events, it can pull the discussion and thinking toward past experiences rather than present perceptions. It can also sometimes make you appear loose in revealing confidences and, thus, less trustworthy.

So, if you conclude through a risk-benefit analysis that self-disclosure will assist the client, try to minimize the risks and maximize the benefits by considering a number of factors. Be sure that your experience is really analogous and that it relates to a significant issue. Minimize the use of self-disclosure early in the lawyer-client relationship when you know less about the client and the client has less reason to trust you. Keep the self-disclosure long enough to establish analogy and understanding, but no longer than necessary to communicate that connection to the client. And, above all, remember that a little self-disclosure goes a very long way.

G. Attorney Opinions

Another major issue that sometimes arises in the decisionmaking process is the extent to which the lawyer should give her/his own opinion. The client may ask, "What would you do?" How should the lawyer respond to that request?

When the model of client-centered lawyering was initially proposed, the proponents argued that lawyers should never give their own opinions. However, many commentators criticized that conclusion. If the model is really supposed to respond to the client's needs and the client asks the lawyer for her/his opinion, isn't it a violation of the model, the commentators questioned, to refuse to give an opinion? Later treatments of client-centeredness responded to this criticism and modified their approach to allow lawyers to respond to a client's request for an opinion.

Whatever your decision as to the appropriateness of providing an opinion, there are two cautions to keep in mind. First, if you are going to give your opinion, don't volunteer it too soon. Lawyers often tell their clients what they would do long before the client has ever requested an opinion. The effect is to then force the client into a position of either repudiating the lawyer (by rejecting her/his opinion) or of accepting an opinion that may conflict with what the client otherwise would choose to do.

Second, if you are going to give an opinion, it should, as much as possible, reflect the client's specific values, needs and circumstances. Any opinion should not reflect what you would do for yourself, but rather what you would do if you were the client. Since that kind of projection is such a difficult thing to do, to really walk in the client's shoes, it should serve as another caution before undertaking this substituted decisionmaking process too quickly or too eagerly.

H. Barriers to Effective Counseling

We need to acknowledge that attorney needs may conflict with the needs of our clients. This potential for harm is magnified by the potential for attorney manipulation of clients in the counseling process. We can manipulate our clients by how we present options—even through such aspects as body language. We can manipulate our clients by the order in which we present options or in the value we place on options or in our predictions of their likelihood of success. The first step in the avoidance of this potential for manipulation and its associated harm is the identification of attorney needs that may adversely affect our honesty and neutrality.

Attorneys may have a need for *power*. This may manifest itself through actions by the attorney toward acquisition, possession and control. An oversized need for power may lead to domination and control of the lawyer-client relationship. An undersized need may lead to inappropriate avoidance of confrontation and failure to advocate aggressively for our clients.

Attorneys may also have a need for *achievement*. This need may manifest itself through competitiveness, aggressiveness, independence, and persistence. An oversized need for achievement may lead a lawyer to override client feelings in order to win. An undersized need may lead to inadequate devotion to client goals. All of us got where we are in law school by being achievers. We therefore need to be especially conscious of the negative aspects of wanting to achieve.

The need for *association* is another attorney need that can affect the counseling process. This need encompasses the lawyer's need for meaningful involvement with others. An oversized need may result in too conciliatory a manner in dealing with adversaries. Our desire to be liked in our initial lawyering experiences may lead us to not be zealous in our advocacy on behalf of our clients. An undersized need may lead to gruffness, insensitivity, impatience, and intolerance. Civility may be sacrificed for no good reason and sometimes with negative effects on the way our clients and their situations are perceived.

There is also the attorney need for *order*. This need may be reflected in neatness, routine, organization, and desire for normalcy. An oversized need may result in inadequate responsiveness to client exigencies and may lead to oversimplification and pigeonholing to avoid personal discomfort. An undersized need may lead to sloppiness, missed deadlines, and inadequate preparation. While a glance at your sock drawer might lead one to conclude that an oversized need is hardly your problem, effective lawyers must maintain their calendar and files scrupulously while embracing the uncertainty that is part of the life of any lawyer.

There is also the potential that attorney *values* may distort the counseling process. We need to be wary of how our values may affect our relationships with our clients. A lawyer who is morally opposed to divorce may present the option of divorce in a manner that unfairly weighs against that option. We need to identify any of our values relevant to our client or to their legal problems. We can then decide if we can transcend our beliefs in order to provide even-handed representation to our client or, if our beliefs will necessarily intrude on the lawyer-client relationship, to withdraw from representation.

Finally, attorneys often want to look like a hero to their clients and therefore unrealistically assess the likelihoods of success of particular options. For example, an attorney may understate the likelihood of success of an option in order to encourage a settlement. Because the client believes that the likelihood of success is less than it really is, the client agrees to accept a settlement offer that is less favorable to the client than the client might otherwise achieve.

Some courts have held that a malpractice action lies against an attorney who recommends a settlement that is unreasonable to the client. In these cases, a trial within the trial is conducted by the court—a trial of the "settled" case within the malpractice action. Damages are based on the difference between what was accepted in settlement and what would likely have been received had the underlying matter gone forward to trial. These malpractice actions are a powerful reminder of the importance of recognizing and compensating for attorney needs that can lead to a manipulation of the counseling process.

I.   Transference and Counter-Transference

Another powerful potential barrier in the counseling process is the possibility of transference and counter-transference. Although we may think that this is solely the province of therapists, the intimacy of the legal counseling relationship and the extent to which clients open up their lives to us make this possibility a potential factor in many attorney-client relationships.

Transference refers to the client's irrational projections onto the counselor of attitudes and associations derived from the client's emotionally significant past relationships. Counter-transference refers to the counselor's irrational projections onto the client of attitudes and associations derived from the counselor's emotionally significant past relationships. Both transference and counter-transference can distort the counseling process and lead lawyer and client to make poor decisions. While the complexities of these projections make it difficult to describe here, we should at least be aware of this potential, especially when lawyer and/or client experience emotional reactions out of proportion to the issues being discussed. And, while we are talking about it, we should also be conscious of the ways that transference and counter-transference can complicate the supervisor-student relationship as well.

J.   A Process Worth the Effort

"Client-centered" counseling takes a great deal of effort. It is far easier to tell a client what to do or to manipulate the process in order to lead a client to select the predetermined choice(s). It also seems to take more attorney time, a critical issue for lawyers in most practices. More thought and preparation is also required to counsel a client honestly and effectively.

So, if it takes more time, thought, and energy to utilize a "client-centered" model of counseling, why should you bother to complicate your professional life? Ultimately, you will have to decide whether to embrace this model in your professional career. However, we believe that there are many reasons why it is worth the trouble.

Client-centered counseling results in better options—options that more accurately reflect the values and goals of our clients. Through client-centered counseling, clients are more likely to invest in their cases and be more effective participants in the advocacy process. And, client-centered counseling is ultimately more cost-effective in designing and implementing courses of action to pursue.

You will ultimately have to decide if these observations are correct. However, your clinic experience provides you with a wonderful laboratory to try out this model. We hope you will try it on for size while critically reflecting on its strengths and weaknesses.

Chapter 12

Negotiation

Most of us negotiate every day of our lives. We negotiate when we make such large purchases as a house or a car and we negotiate more frequently over the smaller details of life. We negotiate with our partners over what to cook for dinner or at what restaurant to eat. We negotiate with our friends over what movie to see or whose car to drive to the show. Earlier in our lives we negotiated with our parents over our allowance and our curfew and over what punishment should be imposed when that curfew was violated.

Surely, even if we were wrong about knowing how to interview or counsel effectively before we started clinic, we must have learned how to negotiate effectively by now. And yet, we sometimes end up eating with our partner at a restaurant at which neither of us wanted to eat. Or, we end up seeing a movie with friends that we hoped to avoid. And, despite our best efforts, we were often "grounded" by our parents for lengths of time far in excess of what should have been imposed.

In this chapter we will discuss some of the significant and growing body of research and theory on effective negotiation skills. There has been a great deal written about the techniques for negotiating effectively, much of it setting forth the kinds of rules about which we have learned to be skeptical. Instead, we will focus on the numerous places in the negotiating process at which choice opportunities are presented. Reflective practitioners need to be able to identify these opportunities and to use them effectively to advance the goals of their clients.

A. Negotiation and ADR

An increasing level of professional and public attention has been paid recently to the concept of ADR or "Alternative Dispute Resolution." Nearly every court and many administrative agencies in the United States (and throughout the world) have imposed mandatory alternative dispute resolution or have so strongly promoted these procedures that they have effectively become mandatory. The goal of such ADR, according to advocates, is to make the resolution of disputes faster, cheaper, and often less emotionally costly.

There are many circumstances in which it is appropriate to resolve disputes through procedures other than decision after a trial by a judge or administrative hearing officer. However, this is not a case of "one size fits all." There are many types of disputes and, even more important, many clients for whom these "alternative" procedures simply do not work. These clients may have goals that cannot be realized through alternative dispute resolution or they may not be able to effectively protect their interests in alternative dispute resolution procedures.

We will therefore think of ADR as standing not for *alternative* dispute resolution, but rather for *appropriate* dispute resolution—a process of matching specific dispute resolution procedures to our clients and their goals. For some of our clients, mediation or arbitration or other forms of "alternative" dispute resolution may be appropriate. For other clients, we will need to resist pressures imposed by courts or administrative tribunals to settle disputes without resort to the full range of judicial or administrative mechanisms available.

Assessment of what is an appropriate dispute resolution process for our clients depends on our identifying with our clients their true needs and objectives. For example, a chance to tell his/her story may be more important to a client than actually "winning" a case. Trying to achieve a long-term goal of proving innocence may be far more important to a client than achieving the short-term goal of avoiding incarceration. This connection between goal and process highlights the important role that effective counseling plays in effective negotiation.

B.   Importance of Negotiation Skills

Whether we are providing representation in a civil case or a criminal matter or in civil and criminal aspects of the same dispute, the fact is that negotiated settlements (settlements short of a full trial of a dispute) are increasingly the norm. Nearly all civil cases end in a negotiated settlement prior to trial, but after discovery and motions (such as motions for partial or full summary judgment). Nearly all criminal cases end in a negotiated settlement (plea bargain) prior to trial, but after discovery and initial motions (such as motions to suppress evidence). Nearly all transactional representation requires multiple negotiations over a range of goods and services, often with numerous other parties. Being able to negotiate effectively on behalf of a client is therefore usually far more important today than being able to conduct a devastating cross-examination or to present a galvanizing closing argument.

C. Expanding our Negotiating Goals

Even those lawyers who understand the importance of negotiating often fail to negotiate effectively because their goals are too narrow. They focus on negotiation solely as an opportunity to reach a settlement—a joint decision with another party that provides the greatest possible benefit to their client. In approaching negotiating from such a narrow perspective, they miss the opportunity to achieve other important goals and also limit their ability to negotiate effectively towards a settlement.

To avoid this trap, we will look at negotiation through a wide lens. Not every negotiation will be successful and even those negotiations that culminate in a settlement do not always result in a settlement on the first attempt. The negotiating process can serve as an opportunity to obtain information about the other side's preparation, theory of the case, evidence, witnesses, and competence. If we fail to use the negotiating process in this way, we do so at our (and our clients') expense. We will fail to obtain information that can help us reach a more favorable negotiated settlement. And, we will fail to obtain information that we can use in a trial or other proceeding if negotiating proves unsuccessful.

D. What Is Information?

Information in a particular negotiation is *anything* that relates in *any* conceivable way to the matter being bargained or to the parties to the bargaining (both principals and their legal representatives). We will want to know the "facts" that our opponents intend to rely on, their assessments of the strengths and weaknesses of their cases, the scope and results of their factual investigations, the scope and results of their legal research, and their goals and their identification of priorities within these goals. All of these types of information may seem fairly obvious since this information goes directly to the evaluation of a case.

There are also other, perhaps less obvious, information needs that we will try to address through the negotiating process. We will try to obtain information as to the way that the opposing lawyers are being compensated and if there any limits on this compensation. We will try to learn the resources that opposing counsel have at their disposal. We will attempt to gain information about opposing counsel's competence in both substantive law and lawyering skills. We will try to identify the personal values of opposing counsel and the ways that these values may affect their representation in this matter. Anything that goes to their valuation of their case and anything that goes to the other side's ability to realize that valuation is fair game for our efforts to obtain information.

To obtain this needed information we will have to, above all, pay attention. Every verbal and non-verbal clue can provide us with information. Receiving and processing these clues is both exhausting and intense. We will need to pay attention to everything that does and does not occur and we will need to do that over an extended period of time. Negotiation is truly a stage at which stamina and fitness are well-rewarded.

E. Negotiation Builds on Interviewing and Counseling Skills

At each lawyering stage so far, we have built on the skills necessary in each prior stage. We will do so again in negotiating as we add strategy, persuasion, and conciliation to our lawyering arsenal. However, before we discuss these new skills, it is important to revisit the place of counseling in the negotiation process.

Effective negotiation depends on effective counseling. Through effective counseling, we help our clients make decisions. We help our clients accurately assess alternatives in light of their associated legal, economic, psychological, and social consequences. We concretely value those predicted consequences and we help our clients choose among alternatives.

If we do a poor job in this counseling process, we will be left with negotiating authority or settlement instructions that may be unrealistic. Or, we may end up negotiating towards a settlement that will not have a chance of achieving our client's real goals. In either instance, effective negotiation will be impossible. So, assuming that we did effectively counsel our clients, we will now turn to choices that must be made in every negotiation.

F. Initiating Negotiations

If negotiations are going to occur, someone must make a decision to start bargaining. There are several options. Negotiations can be initiated by the client, by the lawyer, by the opposing side or opposing counsel, or by the court or other tribunal. Among these various possible actors, who should make the decision as to whether negotiations should be undertaken? We start to answer this question by first looking at the relevant ethical provisions.

Rule 1.2(a) of the ABA Model Rules of Professional Conduct provides that:

> A lawyer *shall abide* by a client's decisions concerning the *objectives* of representation . . . and *shall consult* with the client as to the *means* by which they are to be pursued. A lawyer shall abide by a client's decision whether to accept an offer of settlement of a matter. In a criminal case, the lawyers shall abide by the client's decision, after consultation with the lawyer, as to a plea to be entered, whether to waive jury trial and whether the client will testify. [Emphasis added.]

Negotiating is traditionally viewed as a *means* by which client goals can be achieved. Just like litigation, it is a technique—a tool—and not an end in itself. It should therefore be classified as a lawyer decision, right? Well, maybe not always.

If one of our client's objectives is to "have her day in court," then negotiating would necessarily prevent the achievement of that goal. Therefore, while many (if not most) lawyers would not hesitate to initiate negotiations on their own (even without satisfying the requirement of consultation), in our client-centered model we will involve our client in making the decision to negotiate beyond the limited ethical mandate of consultation.

G.   The Place of the Client

Should you bring your client with you to the negotiation? There is nothing that says that negotiating must be done solely between representatives for the parties. Parties can be and frequently are present throughout the negotiating process. So, how should you and your client approach the question of client presence in negotiations?

Having clients present can be extremely helpful. Clients can provide us with information during the negotiation (or during breaks in the process) that will be helpful to us in assessing communications from our opponent. Having clients present can help them understand the true value of their case by allowing them to hear firsthand the other side's theories and arguments. Having clients present can potentially allow us to reach settlements when offers are made that are not encompassed within our bargaining authority. If our client is a more effective individual than his/her counterpart, this may increase the value of our case in the eyes of our opponent.

However, there are important downsides to having a client present. Sometimes, clients can become emotional during negotiations in ways that are unproductive or even counter-productive. Sometimes, the mere presence of our client can force us to respond to statements made by an adversary that we would otherwise choose to ignore. If our client is easily intimidated, his/her mere presence at the negotiation may cause him/her to accept a settlement offer that is less favorable than could otherwise be achieved.

So, should clients be present or not? The answer, like so many choices in practice, is, "It depends."

H. Choosing a Location

Should you negotiate on your home turf or in the office of your adversary or in some neutral site? Like most of the questions we have addressed in clinic, there is no absolute answer here.

Generally, people feel most comfortable on their home turf and therefore may be able to negotiate more effectively there. However, your office setting may provide valuable information to your opponent that may affect its suitability. Is your office small, dingy, and/or chaotic? If so, it may encourage your opponent to underestimate your ability to pursue a matter if negotiations prove unsuccessful. As a result, it may be harder to reach a settlement favorable to your client. If your office sends a different message to your opponent, it may encourage a settlement more favorable to your client.

Likewise, you may be able to learn useful things about your opponent and his/her practice by negotiating in his/her office. Even sitting in the waiting room can give you a sense of the telephone traffic, about the books in the library, and about the staff in the office. All of these pieces of information are useful in assessing your opponent.

I. Making the Initial Contact

Negotiations may be initiated by telephone or by letter. Both have advantages and disadvantages. Raising the possibility of negotiations in a telephone conversation means that opposing counsel will have to react more spontaneously than if s/he receives a letter proposing negotiations. Raising the possibility of negotiations in a letter means that you will have an opportunity to frame the issues in a more studied and thoughtful way. You will not have to react spontaneously to remarks and positions put forward by your opponent.

Should you initiate negotiations or wait for your opponent to initiate negotiations? The traditional wisdom is that the party initiating negotiations has made the first concession and is therefore starting from a position of weakness. After all, the proposal of negotiations is, in itself, a type of concession. However, the issue of whether or not to initiate negotiations is far more complex. While proposing negotiations may be a sign of weakness, we will be far more sophisticated in our analysis.

The party who initiates negotiations may be able to define the scope of the negotiations and the "playing field" on which those negotiations will take place. Initiating negotiations may give us an opportunity to define the time and ground rules for negotiating. Control of these choices may have a far more significant influence on the bargaining outcome than the question of which side approached the other first. These advantages may more than compensate for any perceived weakness associated with initiating negotiations.

J. In Person or by Telephone

Should you conduct negotiations in person or by telephone? If you are a good observer, in-person negotiations will provide you with an opportunity to observe and interpret clues from the proxemics (the body language) of the other side. In a telephone conversation, you will be limited to the words of the other side and their paralinguistics (the variations in *how* they say what they are saying).

If you can establish a personal connection with opposing counsel through personal contact, you may be able to use that connection to obtain a more favorable settlement for your client. However, if you are a distance apart, negotiations in person may be impossible. And, if you not able to maintain a good "poker face," negotiations by telephone may be preferable.

K. Planning and Preparation

We need to begin our planning and preparation by identifying our client's goals and needs as disclosed during our counseling sessions. We need to master the results of our factual investigation and legal research. Once that process is completed, we can determine the context(s) in which the negotiation will take place. And, we can plan the strategies and styles we will use in the negotiation.

L. Determining the Context for the Negotiation

Negotiations can take place in a *distributive* or in an *integrative* bargaining context. In a *distributive* bargaining context, each party's gain must occur at the expense of the other party. In other words, a pure conflict of interest exists between the parties; it is a "zero-sum game." Most often this occurs when the parties are deciding how to divide a fixed quantity of resources. One party wants to buy a car for as little as possible; the other party wants to sell the car for as much as possible. Every time the purchaser saves $1 on the purchase price of the car, the seller loses $1 of potential profit. Likewise, if the seller obtains a dollar more in sale price, the purchaser necessarily pays one dollar more for the car. Or, two parties might be negotiating over custody of a child. If both parties want sole physical and legal custody of the child, it is impossible for either party to prevail except at the expense of the other.

By contrast, an integrative bargaining context exists when the parties' interests are not directly in conflict—a "win-win" outcome is possible. Agreements are possible in which the level of satisfaction of one party is not necessarily inversely related to that of the other party. For example, two parents may share as their primary goal the best interests of a child. They may conclude that the child's best interests (and, therefore, their goals) will be best served by sharing custody and by maintaining as normal a parental relationship as possible. Similarly, a manufacturer dealing with a supplier may conclude that bargaining for the lowest price on a piece of equipment is less important than maintaining a good relationship with the supplier so that the manufacturer will receive higher quality products during the course of an ongoing business relationship and will receive priority in the event of a supply shortage in the future.

It is also important to remember that characterizations of bargaining contexts (as either integrative or distributive) are not necessarily etched in stone. It may be possible (and it is usually desirable) to try to convert a distributive context into an integrative context. A corporate raider may initially plan to purchase a company in order to dismantle it and sell it off in pieces. If the current owners want to keep the company alive as a single entity, the corporate raider can only succeed at the expense of the current owners. This therefore represents a classic distributive bargaining context.

However, the corporate raider might instead decide to pool money, expertise and political power with the current owners. In this way, the company can grow and thereby generate significant sums for all involved. The "win-lose" scenario is transformed into a "win-win" scenario; the distributive bargaining context is transformed into an integrative context.

We also sometimes mischaracterize a bargaining context because we fail to obtain sufficient information about the goals of the parties. In a distributive bargaining context, the central needs of the parties are in conflict. However, picture the following scenario: A parent is faced with two children who both want a single piece of golden cake with chocolate frosting. We would tend to respond almost automatically by assuming that both children want the cake and that the "Solomonic" solution is to divide the cake in half.

But, it is also possible that we have misinterpreted the goals of the children. Perhaps one child wants the golden cake and doesn't like icing, especially chocolate frosting. Perhaps the other child is primarily interested in the chocolate icing and views the golden cake solely as a means to get to the icing. Under those circumstances, it is possible to transform this negotiation into an integrative model and fully satisfy the needs of both parties by giving one child the cake and the other child the icing.

M. Strategy-Style Combination

After we determine the context or contexts in which the negotiation will take place, we need to determine our strategy-style combination for the negotiation. *Strategy* refers to the plan or approach going on inside your head; *style* refers to the behaviors and attitudes visible to the adverse party. Strategy is invisible to the other party while style is intended to be recognized and processed by the adverse party as a means of furthering our goals for the negotiation. Strategy encompasses the conceptual approach adopted by the negotiator, from planning through implementation, to achieve the underlying goals of the client. Style considers the interpersonal behavior of the negotiator and how that behavior affects the negotiation process.

Just as there are two kinds of contexts in which a negotiation can take place, so there are two types of strategies and two types of styles that can be employed in a negotiation. A negotiator can use an adversarial or a problem-solving strategy and a negotiator can use a competitive or a cooperative style.

1.   Choosing a Strategy

An adversarial strategy consists of tactics intended to undermine the other negotiator's confidence in his/her bargaining position. While an adversarial strategy can be used in both distributive and integrative contexts, when used in an integrative context it ignores opportunities to devise solutions to benefit both parties. A problem-solving strategy consists of those tactics which the negotiator uses when s/he believes that her/his client's interests will be best served by seeking an agreement which is fair and just to both parties, and by developing a relationship with the other party that is based upon trust and good will.

Adversarial negotiators concentrate on creating and defending positions along a bargaining continuum. Problem-solvers focus on identifying needs and brainstorming to develop solutions for mutual gains. Adversarials engage in positional argument. Problem-solvers tend to explore interests. Adversarials make offers to which they appear committed. Problem-solvers advance proposals that invite opponents to accept, reject, or modify based on how the proposals intersect with their interests.

Adversarials are likely to restrict information flow. Problem-solvers are likely to facilitate the exchange of data. Adversarials reject their opponents' offers summarily and make concessions along a continuum. Problem-solvers explain why solutions are acceptable or unacceptable in whole or in part based on a needs analysis.

Problem-solving approaches have the potential advantage of identifying solutions for mutual gain that are likely to bring greater satisfaction to the parties. Effective problem-solving is also easier to implement, less dependent on flawless execution, and more related to careful attention to the needs and interests of the parties.

However, problem-solving approaches can have disadvantages. It is almost impossible to use a problem-solving approach in a setting in which the parties are bargaining over a single fungible item. Problem-solving approaches also tend to take more time to implement and may thrust the parties into ongoing relationships that will be discomforting to the parties.

2. Selecting a Style

A competitive style consists of behaviors designed to undermine the opposing negotiator's confidence in his/her bargaining position. The goal of a competitive style is to induce the opponent to enter into an agreement less advantageous to her/his client than s/he would have agreed to prior to the negotiation. Competitive behaviors include high demands, threats, and arguments.

A cooperative style is premised on the notion that when one party displays behavior that is fair, reasonable and accommodating, the other party is likely to respond in kind. Cooperative behaviors include reasonable opening offers. Cooperative negotiators make arguments based on what is fair and just. They also make concessions to encourage the other negotiator to reciprocate.

Effective competitive negotiators are dominating, forceful, attacking, aggressive, ambitious, clever, honest, perceptive, analytical, convincing, and self-controlled. By contrast, effective cooperative negotiators are trustworthy, fair, honest, courteous, personable, tactful, sincere, perceptive, reasonable, convincing, and self-controlled.

Newer lawyers often mistake a cooperative style for a "polite" competitive style. A lawyer need not scream or curse or threaten in order to negotiate competitively. Just like the song "Never smile at a crocodile," it is very possible to be amiable and have a pleasant demeanor while cutting an opponent to ribbons. So, don't be taken in by a toothsome grin 'cause you never know what's going on inside his (or her) skin.

3.   Factors to Consider in Choosing a Strategy-Style

You will need to choose the negotiating strategy and style that is most appropriate to your particular negotiation in light of your client's goals, needs, and resources, the issues involved, your client's comfort level with specific strategy-style combinations, and your opponent's strategy-style. That means that you will need to be able to negotiate in more than one strategy-style combination. It is no answer to say that you feel most comfortable negotiating in a problem-solving, cooperative strategy-style combination if that is not the combination best suited to achieving your client's goals. You will have to become comfortable with and effective in multiple combinations—adapting your choices to the specific negotiation (and occasionally to the specific issue within that negotiation).

You will need to first consider the goals of your client and those of the opposing party. If getting as much as possible of a limited commodity is the goal, you should consider an adversarial competitive strategy-style. If a continuing relationship is an important goal, you should consider a problem-solving cooperative strategy-style.

You will also need to consider the configuration of needs of both your client and the other party. Are these needs shared by the parties? Or, are the needs of one party independent of those of the other? Do the needs of the parties conflict? If needs do not conflict, you should consider a problem-solving cooperative strategy-style. If needs conflict, you should consider an adversarial competitive strategy-style.

You will also need to consider the resources available to each side to potentially fight a war of attrition—a battle in which the parties wear each other down through motions, discovery, and similar maneuvers. How much money, personnel, and time are available to your client and to the opposing party? If client resources are more limited, you should consider a problem-solving cooperative strategy-style. If client resources are more unlimited, you can better afford to utilize an adversarial-competitive strategy-style.

Next, you will need to consider the issues involved in the negotiation. Can the parties creatively generate additional issues to expand the subject matter of the negotiation? If issues are fairly numerous, you should consider a problem-solving cooperative strategy-style. If issues are fairly limited, you should consider an adversarial-competitive strategy-style.

You will need to also consider the behaviors that are likely to be visible to your client in each of the strategy-style combinations. You will need to consider the comfort/discomfort your client may experience if you utilize a competitive versus a cooperative bargaining style. If your client will feel uncomfortable with a competitive style, you should consider a cooperative style.

You will also need to consider the strategy-style choices of your opponent, a critical piece of information you will need to obtain early in the negotiating process. Some lawyers are typecast early in their practices and always attempt to rely on intimidation while others shy away from anything threatening. You will need to find out what you can about your opponent in advance of the negotiation, but constantly be willing to test these characterizations as the negotiating process moves forward. If your opponent utilizes an adversarial-competitive combination, it is difficult (but not impossible) to respond effectively with a problem-solving-cooperative combination.

Finally, you will need to remember that the strategy-style choice can be issue-specific. Even if you utilize an adversarial-competitive strategy-style on one issue, you may still be able to utilize a problem-solving cooperative approach on another issue. Therefore, even after you consider an overall bargaining model, you will need to consider the extent to which a different strategy or style should be utilized to address a specific issue.

4.   Interplay of Strategy and Style

Although we have tended to link a problem-solving strategy with a cooperative style (and an adversarial strategy with a competitive style), it is possible to utilize any of the four strategy-style combinations. Thus, we can choose among (and try to place our opponent in) any of the four quadrants below:

	Adversarial Strategy	**Problem-Solving Strategy**
Competitive Style	Rigid positions, hard bargaining	Limited consideration of needs and objectives
Cooperative Style	Concessions and compromise	Open consideration of needs and solutions

N. Obtaining and Assessing Information

Some authors identify the obtaining and assessing of information as a separate stage in the negotiating process. This is done in order to emphasize the importance of this focus. However, because information is sought and obtained and blocked and leaked throughout the entire negotiating process, we will not identify it as a separate stage. But, we will also not lose sight of its importance in the negotiating process.

You will need to carefully evaluate the style and substance of your opponents' communications. What are they saying and what are they not saying? What information are they providing and what information are they guarding? What non-verbal clues can help you decode their statements and other actions?

As we discussed earlier, information in a particular negotiation is anything that relates in any conceivable way to the matter being bargained or to the parties to the bargaining (both principals and their legal representatives). In order to prepare for obtaining information through your negotiation, you will need to plan for each of the tasks of getting information, giving information, and guarding information. While information is supposed to flow freely in a problem-solving cooperative model, control of information is especially critical in an adversarial competitive negotiation.

You will begin offensively by identifying the information you know, the information you need to confirm, and the information you need to obtain. From a defensive posture, you will need to identify the information you must protect from the other side. Finally, you must identify the information you are willing to give, especially as part of an effort to "loosen" up your opponent and thereby encourage him/her to provide you with information you need.

Direct information probes tend to work poorly in an adversarial competitive negotiation. The lack of subtlety puts the opposing side on notice and makes your information priorities too obvious. You will therefore use many of the techniques you first used in interviewing—broad, open-ended questions with active listening techniques to encourage your opponents to talk (and leak information) naturally (and carelessly).

Information probes are sometimes useful to confirm points and they may be used against us to put us on the spot. In such a situation, we need to be conscious of the responses employed by our opponent and we need to prepare to effectively block direct probes seeking information we want to protect. There are a number of techniques that are commonly employed in such circumstances, but each technique has at least some cost associated with it.

You can answer a question with a question ("What do you want to do about this?" "Well, what do you want to do?"). You can over-answer a question with more information than it reasonably seeks in order to obscure the relevant information. You can under-answer the question with less information than it reasonably seeks and thereby appear to respond without really answering the question. You can answer a different question from the one asked as if you misunderstood the question. You can ignore the question and keep on talking (as if you really did not hear the question that was asked). Or, as a last resort, you can treat the question as inappropriate and rule it "out-of-bounds" and avoid answering at all. However, in doing so, you may thereby emphasize the importance of the information sought.

If you are going to directly answer a question, you need to remember that an honest answer may provide an opponent with leverage and information to use against you and your client. However, a dishonest answer may give rise to ethical problems and may undercut credibility. Meanwhile, an evasive answer reduces risk and may be the only alternative in an adversarial model.

Rule 4.1 of the ABA Model Rules of Professional Conduct governs truthfulness in statements to others. It provides that:

> In the course of representing a client, a lawyer shall not knowingly:
>
> (a) make a false statement of material fact or law to a third person; or
>
> (b) fail to disclose a material fact to a third person when disclosure is necessary to avoid assisting a criminal or fraudulent act by a client, unless disclosure is prohibited by Rule 1.6.

The Comments to Rule 4.1 further provide that:

> A misrepresentation can occur if the lawyer incorporates or affirms a statement of another person that the lawyer knows is false. . . .

Whether a particular statement should be regarded as one of fact can depend on the circumstances. Under generally accepted conventions in negotiation, certain types of statements ordinarily are not taken as statements of material fact. Estimates of price or value placed on the subject of a transaction and a party's intentions as to an acceptable settlement of a claim are in this category . . . .

One of the questions left unaddressed by the Model Rule is the extent to which evasion should be viewed as indistinguishable from misrepresentation? The United States Supreme Court provided at least one answer to this question in its 1972 decision in *Bronston v. United States*.

In *Bronston*, the defendant had been convicted of perjury for answers provided to creditors in a bankruptcy proceeding. As framed by the Court, the question was "whether a witness may be convicted of perjury for an answer, under oath, that is literally true but not responsive to the questions asked and arguably misleading by negative implication." The Supreme Court answered this question in the negative and unanimously reversed the conviction. Writing for the Court, Chief Justice Burger wrote that evasion is not the same as lying. Relations between lawyers, he noted, are at arms length. "[A]ny special problems arising from the literally true but unresponsive answer," the Chief Justice emphasized, "are to be remedied through the 'questioner's acuity.'" You are therefore well-warned to listen carefully in negotiations to determine if the other person actually answered your questions.

O. Persuading Opponents

Much of negotiation is targeted at persuading people to do things that they would not otherwise do. We negotiate in order to persuade a prosecuting attorney to not file charges against our client or to not pursue charges once filed. We negotiate in order to persuade an adverse party to not sue our client or to accept lesser relief than they might otherwise want. We negotiate in order to persuade a potential business partner to contract with our client on terms that are more favorable to our client than might otherwise be offered. In all of these settings our goal is to manipulate the decisionmaking process of someone who controls decisions that can affect the achievement of the goals identified by our clients.

There are some bottom lines to effective negotiating. In order to successfully conclude a negotiation, at least one party to a negotiation must be persuaded if a dispute is to be settled or an agreement concluded. To have a negotiation, at least one factor must be drawing the parties together. At the same time, at least one factor must be keeping them apart.

P.   Interplay of Persuasion and Strategy

Adversarial negotiators try to persuade opponents to view the matters at issue most favorably to them. Cooperative negotiators try to persuade opponents to appreciate their world and to understand how that world relates to that of their opponent. There are four techniques that are used to persuade: arguments, appeals, threats, and promises. We will address each of these techniques in turn.

1.   Argument

An argument is the presentation of reasons and supporting authority to justify a negotiation position or to rebut an adversary's position. A good argument (like a good story) needs to be sufficiently detailed, balanced, focused, and appropriately emotionally appealing. An argument appeals to your opponent's rational sense.

In order to build a persuasive argument, you need to first identify a normative standard. Then you must demonstrate how the normative standard applies to the issue in question. Finally, you must demonstrate how the normative standard either advances your cause or counters the reasoning of your opponent.

2.   Appeal

An appeal is a request made of an adversary for a gratuitous concession. Whereas an argument is inherently rational, an appeal is necessarily irrational or at least "arational." It relies on persuasive approaches that are strictly personal or emotional in nature. The power of an appeal in fact varies directly with the power of the emotions unleashed. As explained by Lord Henry in Oscar Wilde's THE PICTURE OF DORIAN GRAY (1891), "The advantage of the emotions is that they lead us astray." However, an appeal may send a message to an opponent that your arguments are relatively weak and that you are therefore trying to invoke sympathy for your client's position.

3.   Threats and Promises

Threats and promises are two sides of the same persuasive coin. A threat necessarily plays on an opponent's fears. By contrast, a promise plays on an opponent's desires. A threat will be successful if a threatened opponent can be made to understand that it will be less costly to comply with our demands than it will be to suffer the damage that would follow if we carried out the threat. A promise will succeed if the offer is sufficiently attractive to encourage one party to relinquish his/her demands in order to receive the promised benefit.

Threats tend to be a common feature of adversarial competitive negotiations. Thoughtless or impulsive negotiators threaten out of frustration, not because they have carefully analyzed the benefits and costs of making a threat. Ineffective negotiators threaten when they are not prepared to follow through on their threats and then have their bluff called.

To the extent that you decide that threats are a necessary part of your negotiating arsenal, you need to plan for the potential use of threats. You need to identify what our opponent fears most. You then need to determine how to effectively threaten your opponent with that outcome.

You will also need to plan to defend against the potential use of threats by your opponents. You will need to identify what you fear most. And, you will need to decide how to respond if you are threatened with that outcome.

In order to be effective, a threat must be communicated. It must be understood as a threat by the recipient. The outcome threatened must be valued by the recipient or it will not raise the specter of sufficient costs to encourage the opponent to yield. The threat must be credible and believed by the recipient. It also must be prospective; it cannot relate to an event that has already occurred.

Like responding to an information probe, there are several options for responding to a threat. The recipient can claim the threat has no value or that the threat has already been implemented and therefore whatever costs might be suffered have already been incurred. The target might also misunderstand the threat or ignore it. The threatened party might also treat the threat with humor, not taking it seriously. Or, the threat might be responded to with a threat, a strategy of escalation. Finally, like the approach of ruling a question out of bounds, the recipient might treat the threat as a breach of etiquette and thereby take it off the negotiating table.

Threats are negative rewards, while promises are positive rewards. To which type of reward is the opponent more likely to respond? Threats tend to be utilized by adversarial competitive negotiators; promises tend to be utilized by cooperative problem-solving negotiators.

4. Threats and Extortion

A special subset of threats includes those threats involving criminal charges or disciplinary charges. A government attorney in a welfare over-payment case may threaten the filing of welfare fraud charges in order to persuade a recipient to accept a finding of overpayment and sign a confession of judgment. A private attorney may threaten opposing counsel with disciplinary charges if s/he does not accept a settlement offer less favorable to her/his client.

Rule 8.4 of the ABA Model Rules of Professional Conduct arguably includes the threat of criminal or disciplinary charges within the kinds of actions that constitute professional misconduct. However, many state rules of professional conduct eliminate any ambiguity and explicitly declare such conduct to be unethical. However, these rules do not necessarily identify when such conduct comes within the ethical prohibition.

In the District of Columbia, for example, Rule 8.4 goes beyond the text of the ABA Model Rule in defining "professional misconduct" to include actions by a lawyer to "seek or threaten to seek criminal charges or disciplinary charges solely to obtain an advantage in a civil matter." The conduct that comes within this ethical prohibition is not always easy to define, however. When are charges sought *solely* to obtain an advantage? Does the mere mention of criminality of conduct violate this rule as, for example, when a lawyer in a divorce action mentions the apparent underreporting of income on a tax return? Since income is relevant to alimony and child support, it is hard to conclude that the reference is made *solely* to gain an advantage. And, the reference to possible criminal conduct may create the specter of a criminal prosecution without actually constituting the seeking (or threat of seeking) criminal charges.

As the following cartoon indicates, this distinction is also not well understood by the general public. Every lawsuit constitutes a threat of one sort or another. However, it is only those threats involving criminal charges to gain an advantage in a civil proceeding that even arguably come within the ethical prohibition.

Q. Getting Down to Real Bargaining

Without effective control of information and productive persuasion, a negotiator is not fully prepared for "real" bargaining. However, additional work is required to effectively prepare for this stage. This is true whether one is negotiating within a distributive or integrative bargaining context and whether one is negotiating with an adversarial-competitive or problem-solving-cooperative strategy-style combination.

The first step in this preparation is to identify and characterize every need of each party. We need to evaluate the relative importance of each need to each party and we need to compare (or contrast) needs of our clients with those of adversaries. Each need must be classified as *essential* (a deal-breaker if it is not obtained) or *important* (should be part of any settlement) or merely *desirable* (get it if you can). Each need must be compared to see if it is *shared* with the other side (if both parties can be satisfied at the same time) or *independent* (if one party's need can be satisfied without the other party suffering some detriment) or *inconsistent* (if both parties cannot be satisfied at the same time). It is obviously easier to reach a settlement if parties share important common needs and if there are no essential inconsistent needs to address. Problem-solving negotiators search for solutions that meet the shared, independent, and conflicting needs and interests of the parties.

R. The Bargaining Continuum

Adversarial negotiators must plan for four categories of moves along the bargaining continuum: the opening offer, the target point, one or more commitment points, and the resistance level. The opening offer is the place along the bargaining continuum at which the parties expect the initial offer to be made and often reflects a decision as to which party is expected to make the opening offer. The target point is the point at which the negotiators expect the settlement to occur. The commitment (or concession) points are the places along the bargaining continuum at which each party gives up something in the hope of getting something. The resistance level is the level beyond which a settlement is no longer possible—the level at which the party is willing to go to trial rather than agree to a negotiated settlement.

The efforts of adversarial negotiators are largely directed at attempting to identify the settlement zone. The settlement zone is the area in which there is overlap between the negotiating authority of one representative and the negotiating authority of the other attorney; it is the area of overlap between the resistance levels of the two parties. If there is no area of overlap, there is no common ground for negotiators to exploit. Under such circumstances, there cannot be a settlement unless new bargaining authority is obtained.

Adversarial negotiators often use bargaining charts to plan their negotiating strategy. In a complex negotiation, one in which there might be multiple issues to negotiate, a bargaining chart will ordinarily be necessary for each such issue to be negotiated. In a very real sense, the purpose of the bargaining chart is to identify the size and location of the settlement zone in which the negotiation can conclude successfully.

A bargaining chart might look something like this:

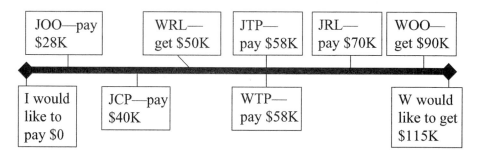

In this negotiation, J is being sued by W. W would like to get $115,000; J would like to pay nothing. At this point they are $115,000 apart. J's opening offer is to pay $28,000; W's opening offer is to receive $90,000. At this point they are $68,000 apart. J's resistance level is paying $70,000; if J has to pay more than $70,000 he would prefer to go to trial. W's resistance level is receiving $50,000; if W receives less than $50,000 he would prefer to go to trial. So, the settlement zone is $20,000 wide, between J paying and W receiving $50,000 and J paying and W receiving $70,000. Both J and W expect the negotiation to end at their target points, $58,000.

Adversarial negotiators set their opening offers beyond both their resistance levels and their target points. Researchers on initial offers in an adversarial negotiation have concluded that a *moderately* high/low opening position in an adversarial negotiation best balances the normally competing desires to maximize the return and to avoid a deadlock. An extremely high opening offer may completely alienate the other side and make a negotiated settlement impossible. Too low an opening offer will result in a settlement far less favorable to that client.

By contrast, problem-solving negotiators operate in a far less linear pattern of negotiation. They discuss needs and explore how to classify and compare those needs. They may put forward multiple, and perhaps conflicting, simultaneous offers to facilitate clarification and elaboration of their opponent's needs through rejection, modification or tentative acquiescence.

Adversarial negotiators respond to the opening offer by rejecting it. This fits the fundamental philosophy of adversarial negotiators: "My way or the highway!" By contrast, problem-solving negotiators respond to any offer with "Yes, and . . . ." This approach fits the fundamental philosophy of problem-solvers: "We must be committed to seeking solutions that meet each other's needs."

Three "rules" have been developed for adversarial offer-making. Any offer must be brief; if you go on too long you run the risk of providing information that will be used by the opposing side against you and your client. Any offer must be specific; if you are too vague, you will not be convincing. And, any offer must be justified; it must include some rationale for that offer and why no further concession is appropriate. Otherwise, since any offer is a form of concession, the offer will be treated as an invitation to make further concessions.

S.   Concessions

Concession is a necessary part of adversarial negotiations. A concession is appropriate when it is required to facilitate movement toward agreement, but it must not do serious damage to the adversarial negotiator's credibility. Every concession by an adversarial negotiator erodes credibility to some extent, but the strategy of never making a concession violates the norms of negotiation.

Concessions do not have the same place or meaning in a problem-solving strategy. Problem-solvers exist in a scattergram world where, by definition, they never concede (as such) but rather move about in search for optimal solutions to maximize mutual gain.

When is it time to make a concession? A concession is appropriate when time is short and a deadline looms or when an opponent has become entrapped and needs some relief in order to move forward. Concessions may also be necessary to preserve a relationship or goodwill or to influence important third parties. And concessions become critical when other tactics (*e.g.*, argument, appeal, threat and promise) have failed.

T.   Impact of the Negotiating Process

As people begin to negotiate, a phenomenon commonly occurs. The more they negotiate, the more the representatives (and sometimes the parties they represent) become invested in achieving a settlement. This can have positive and negative consequences.

On the positive side, people do not want to view their settlement efforts as a waste of time. They are therefore more likely to compromise on more difficult issues and find common ground where none previously seemed possible. This is why negotiators often start with easier issues and leave more difficult issues until the end of the process.

On the negative side, because the investment in the negotiating process may be so great, the negotiators may be willing to agree to compromises that prevent important (and sometimes indispensable) client goals from being achieved. Although the client will ultimately have to approve the settlement, the power of the negotiator to filter information and manipulate the counseling process may result in the client being persuaded to accept a negotiation that is not in his/her best interests.

This phenomenon, that the longer we negotiate the more likely we are to achieve a negotiated settlement because we become more invested in achieving a negotiated settlement, can also be used in mischievous ways by some negotiators. Some adversarial negotiators use the tactic of "sandbagging" to achieve settlements more favorable to their clients. In "sandbagging," a new issue is placed on the table *after* the parties seem to have agreed on a settlement, often as if it had been there all along or had simply been forgotten by the lawyer. Because the parties are invested in the negotiated settlement that they had reached, they agree to all or a significant part of this newly-presented claim.

"Sandbagging" is ordinarily not a part of problem-solving strategies because the parties spend so much time placing their needs on the table as a prelude to searching for common ground. However, it often appears in adversarial negotiations in which negotiators are always searching for even the smallest edge on their opponent. Attorneys must therefore be aware of this phenomenon and be prepared to deal with it in one of several ways.

As with the tactical options for responding to threats or information probes, the target of "sandbagging" can treat the matter as a breach of etiquette and rule it "out of bounds." Or, the target can use this as an opportunity to add additional demands to his/her side of the negotiating scales—to "sandbag" in return. Whether these approaches or some other approach is taken, "sandbagging" is common enough in practice so that it is necessary to prepare for in case it is used against you by an opponent.

U. Closure

In the event that an agreement is reached between the negotiators, the agreement must ordinarily be memorialized in writing. If the negotiators have the bargaining authority to agree to a settlement on behalf of their principals, it may be possible to prepare a memorandum during the negotiation session, even if the memorandum is handwritten. However, more commonly, a comprehensive settlement agreement will be reduced to writing after the negotiation and then signed by the principals to the agreement (and often by their attorneys).

The question of who will draft the agreement is often of critical importance. Even in the most extended negotiations, it is often impossible to anticipate every issue that will need to be reflected in the settlement agreement. It is only in drafting the settlement agreement that one identifies all of the issues that must be addressed. The person who creates the initial draft of the settlement agreement thereby often identifies and defines the terms that will be negotiated over, if necessary, in completing the settlement process.

Chapter 13
Attorney Satisfaction

Over the course of your clinical experience, you have learned a great deal about the skills and values that make for responsible and effective lawyers. You have also had a chance to "try on" your future identity as a lawyer and to begin to define that identity. Hopefully, you have discovered aspects of lawyering that gave you pleasure and that you will want to experience again in practice. And, you may have experienced aspects of lawyering that gave you little satisfaction and that you will want to avoid in practice.

One of our hopes for you is that 5, 10 and 20 years out from your clinical experience (and from law school), you will look back happily on your decision to become a lawyer. Clinic can and should play a role in achieving that outcome by providing you with opportunities to critically reflect on questions of career satisfaction, a topic not often discussed in law school.

And yet, isn't it premature to talk about satisfaction when you have not even graduated from law school and when the focus of so many of your colleagues is on simply getting a first job (any job!) and beginning to pay off law school loans? There are several answers to this question. But, perhaps most telling is the fact that choices made early in your career often strongly influence what will come in the years ahead. And, if you are going to be able to look back on a career with satisfaction, you need to begin to define a lawyering career in which you can do the kinds of work for the kinds of clients in the kinds of settings that will make you happy in your professional career and in your personal life.

A. The Statistics for Too Many

On December 30, 1996, THE WASHINGTON POST published an article by David Segal describing the lives of associates in major Washington law firms. One of the firms profiled was a nationally-prominent and well-respected law firm. Despite its national prominence, in the 1994 survey by THE AMERICAN LAWYER magazine of mid-level associates, it had been rated as Washington's most miserable law firm.

After receiving the results of the 1994 survey, the firm's leaders immediately launched a campaign to make the associates happy. Salaries were boosted by up to $7000 per year, partners were encouraged to communicate better with associates, and a subsidized day care center was established. These efforts succeeded in moving the firm from last to next to last in the annual city-wide survey.

THE WASHINGTONIAN magazine published a more recent article about the lives of lawyers at major law firms in Washington, D.C. This article by Ross Guberman described his short career at one of these firms. He and his fellow associates had been wooed by the firm during law school through an extensive summer "boot camp" featuring sailing on the Chesapeake Bay, barbecues at the homes of partners, and access to beachside retreats. In his article, *Running From the Law*, Guberman described the mass exodus of bright young lawyers within a few years of joining such major law firms. The author pointed to the sky-high salaries, lavish parties and plush offices and asked, "Why Do So Many Young Attorneys Want Out?"

What should we make of these results? What message do these articles send you about your future career as a lawyer? For many of your friends, just getting a first law job and beginning to pay off their debts from law school (and perhaps undergraduate school) really are the main things on their minds. Can't you put off thinking about being happy with your career choices and being satisfied with your future as a lawyer until later? Moreover, what have these lawyers got to be unhappy about? Aren't they making nearly as much to start as a U.S. Supreme Court Justice and more than almost all of the professors who taught them (and you) in law school?

B. The Tyranny of Billable Hours

One of the prime reasons why new lawyers making "big bucks" at major firms are so unhappy is the impact of the *billable* hour. As this cartoon reflects, billable hours are the lifeblood of firm finances, and the pressure to maximize billable hours can be palpable.

At some firms, lawyers seeking to become partner (on the ever-lengthening partner track) are expected to bill 2,400 hours (and more) per year. Associates who are "committed" to the firm and to their career are expected to meet and exceed those limits. While that number may seem meaningless in the

"Remember to round each billable hour off to the nearest week."

abstract, a little applied mathematics can help bring the impact of that number home.

In order to bill even 2,400 hours per year, an associate would have to work approximately 3,200 hours per year (since not every hour can be billed to a client), 3,200 hours per year breaks down to approximately 270 hours per month. Two hundred seventy hours per month breaks down to approximately 63 hours per week. A lawyer working 7 days per week would have to work 9 hours per day to reach that level.

And, these estimates may be conservative. Some commentators have estimated that in order to bill even 2000 billable hours a year, a lawyer would have to work 78 hours per week—11 hours a day, 7 days per week. Even if you could afford to buy a new sports car with your generous salary from the firm, you wouldn't have either very much time or very much energy to enjoy it or much else in life.

C. Work in Other Settings

While the worst press has probably been received by major law firms, many attorneys in government, public interest, and small firm practices are hardly ecstatic over their work lives. They may discover that their practices are far from the work they had anticipated. They may find themselves submerged in paper; they may seldom have the opportunity to pursue the lofty principles that attracted them initially. They also may have discovered that lack of status and lower compensation are not balanced by other benefits of the job. And, overwhelming work hours are not unique to the private sector. Neither are unnecessary levels of conflict and pointless incivility both in litigation settings and in transactional contexts.

D. Developing a Theory of Ourselves

So, are the prospects for your career really as dark as all that? Hardly! Too often lawyers build a career the same way that they practice law—thoughtlessly. They take jobs without really thinking about the relationship between that job and their needs. While large firm jobs may be right for some people and public interest positions right for others, the fit between a particular individual and a particular job may be painful. "One size" often fits nobody. It is therefore no wonder that so many lawyers discover that they are profoundly unhappy with their choices 5 and 10 years out.

Throughout your clinical experience, we have talked about the importance of developing a theory of the client—a set of legal and non-legal strategies or approaches for achieving the various goals of our clients. If client theory is so important in moving from status quo towards achievement of goals, shouldn't we have a theory of ourselves? This next section begins that process.

1. Identifying and Prioritizing

One of the things that we worked hard to achieve with our clients was an accurate identification of their needs and goals and priorities. In the counseling process, we often probed our clients about feelings that were not articulated and confronted them with apparent inconsistencies in their goals.

To the extent that, "What is good for the goose is good for the gander," we should therefore begin with goal, need, and priority clarification on our own part. And, just as we emphasized the importance of honesty on the part of our clients, so we need to be conscious of the importance of being honest with ourselves. So, let's start by identifying some of the needs that many of us bring to our legal careers.

2. Money

How much money do you need to provide yourself with the standard of living (and the level of security) to which you want to become accustomed? It is fairly easy to determine the minimum level of income you will need to meet your costs of shelter, food, clothing, entertainment, and debt load. But, how much money do you need or want beyond that level? And, what tradeoffs in the realization of other goals are you willing to accept in order to achieve that standard of living? Will you be satisfied driving a Taurus or do you "need" to have a BMW in the garage? Will you be satisfied owning a townhouse or do you "need" to have a 4,000 square foot house on an acre of land?

3. Political Agenda

Some people come to the practice of law with a desire to use their law degree to further personal socio-political goals. You may want to lessen the level of discrimination against women in society or to protect the rights of gay, lesbian, bisexual, and transgender persons. You may want to expand the civil rights of minority persons or to change the condition of the poor through legal advocacy. You may want to work to protect civil liberties or to prosecute crime.

If you are driven by the desire to achieve one or more socio-political goals, a career that does not permit you to work at least in significant part towards achievement of those goals will necessarily be less than satisfying. However, if socio-political concerns are not an important part of your makeup, a career in one of these fields that requires you to accept tradeoffs in other areas (like salary) will likely not be acceptable in the long-term.

4. Power

Many persons like the power that they feel as lawyers. Sometimes this power is simply the by-product of being privy to knowledge that is out of the reach of most people. However, sometimes the power comes from associations with clients whose power in their own right rubs off on their legal representatives. By contrast, representing the dispossessed and the disempowered often gives one a frustrating feeling of powerlessness in the justice system. There are other benefits to these practices, but power is not likely to be among them.

If feeling powerful is important to you, this must necessarily be reflected in the clients you choose to represent. That personal "need" acknowledgment dictates certain career choices and excludes certain others. By contrast, if representing the dispossessed and disempowered and occasionally tilting at windmills is important to you, careers in legal services or as a public defender or in public interest law may be far more appropriate.

5. Thrill of the Kill

Many individuals go to law school after having been told by their parents and friends that, "You like to argue so much, you ought to become a lawyer." Does that sound familiar? Or, you may have developed a taste for defeating an opponent in moot court or trial practice experiences. For such individuals, much of the satisfaction of lawyering will be found in adversarial settings, often in trial. If you like the feeling of combat, much of the satisfaction you will find in lawyering will be found in adversarial settings, often in a trial environment. For others, adversarial combat is the last thing they want in their professional lives.

Is "the thrill of the kill" something that you will need from your profession? If so, a career that does not provide you with an opportunity to engage in "battle" will be unlikely to satisfy you. At the same time, are you willing to incur the tradeoffs in terms of stress, demands on time, and disruptiveness in your life that are inherent in that kind of career? Many people who think that they want to be litigators have no idea what the life of a litigator is like or are unaware of the range of legal careers that are possible.

6.   Feeling Good About Your Work

There are many people who feel that they can represent either side in a dispute without difficulty. If retained by a landlord to evict a low-income tenant, they have no qualms about their role in the eviction process so long as they can operate within the bounds of the legal system. For others, evicting a tenant, even after resorting to extensive legal process, would result in significant and unacceptable emotional and other costs.

How important to you is "feeling good about your work?" Can you deal with a relatively neutral emotional canvas by, for example, representing one corporate client against another corporate client or with a canvas in which you are representing a powerful interest (a corporation or the state) against a vulnerable individual? If you can't, then the feeling of being "bought" by a client to further an "immoral" end will tear you up. By contrast, the more you become invested in powerless clients, the more stress and anxiety you are likely to feel regarding your responsibility for the outcomes of your representation; the less invested you are in your clients the less meaningful your work becomes and the easier it becomes to tolerate losses.

7.   Intellectual Challenge

Many people need to face new intellectual challenges every day. Fresh intellectual challenges are essential to their professional satisfaction. However, cost-efficiency is often furthered by limiting oneself to the same or similar kinds of legal work presenting the same or similar issues on behalf of the same or similar client population. If variety is the spice of life, it is often also the spice of higher costs and lower incomes. For other lawyers, working on the same types of matters for the same types of clients is reassuring since they do not have to venture into the unknown and experience the anxiety that often goes along with uncertainty.

How important is it for you to find fresh intellectual challenges in your legal work? Certain practices present practitioners with issues of first impression nearly every day. Other practices are based on almost "routinized" representation of multiple clients with the same legal needs. Even in a "routinized" practice it is still possible to approach each client in a fresh manner (admittedly, that is at the heart of client-centeredness). However, while such an approach will have positive consequences for client outcomes, it may have less favorable consequences for caseload management and productivity screens.

8. Status

There was a time when being a lawyer was an almost universally respected profession. The mere status of "lawyer" cloaked one with an aura of respectability and status. However, more recently, the decision to become a lawyer is more often met with at least jokes and sometimes with derision. As indicated in this cartoon, lawyers often feel a need to apologize or at least explain their choice of professions.

"I am a member of the legal profession, but I'm not a lawyer in the pejorative sense."

Think about the range of lawyer jokes that abound. Nearly every one has heard the joke: "What does one call a cruise ship that sinks with a boatload of lawyers? A good start!" Think about the range of images of lawyers in movies and on television. Against these images, the Abe Lincolns and Atticus Finches seem a distant and somewhat quaint memory.

We also have cartoons like the two below:

NON SEQUITOR © Wiley Miller. Dist. by UNIVERSAL PRESS SYNDICATE. Reprinted with permission. All rights reserved.

In the first, the child must apologize to her parents for having decided to become a lawyer. In the second, the child only becomes a lawyer when he discovers that he cannot realize his first choice.

There are a number of other aspects that go into status. Is it important to you to work in a setting that has oriental rugs on the floor and fine art on the walls? Many public interest lawyers work in settings only slightly better than the environments in which their clients live. Would that be acceptable to you? If not, you need to decide what tradeoffs you are willing to accept to achieve that level of status.

9. Having a Life Outside the Office

How important is it for you to have a life outside the office and to not define yourself solely by your work? It is possible to have one's life consumed by work and to have little time and energy for anything else. If the symphony or sports or friends or reading are important to you, then you will need to define a work experience that will allow you to engage in those activities. However, that may mean excluding certain kinds of careers and accepting certain tradeoffs in order to have the time and energy to enjoy those activities.

10. Being a Responsible Partner in a Relationship

You may be happy to live your life alone and not be part of a relationship. Or, you may need to be a partner in a relationship in order to be satisfied with your life. Being a responsible partner in a relationship requires the commitment of time and energy, time and energy that may be sapped by a job that leaves little of either commodity for you to commit to a relationship. Lawyers and their partners often talk about the physical and mental exhaustion they feel when they come home from work. If this exhaustion is balanced by feelings of professional satisfaction, the toll on personal lives may not be that great. However, in the absence of some level of professional satisfaction, physical and mental exhaustion may doom any relationship. Sexual disinterest and dysfunction are only two of the characteristics that are found in many such pairings.

If being a responsible partner in a relationship is important to you, time and energy must be carved out from your professional life in order to invest in your personal life. However, the decision to not invest everything in your professional life may be perceived as a lack of professional commitment. In work settings in which the employer feels that s/he "owns" you and your time, the result may be termination or at least a lack of promotion.

11. Being a "Good" Parent

This cartoon from the series "Doonesbury" is a wonderful reminder of the tradeoffs that many American families feel. Both parents in this strip have busy careers—Rick Redfern as a reporter and Joanie Caucus as a lawyer. However, the experience of balancing her life as parent and professional has a special resonance for Joanie. Even though Rick fashions himself as a "new age sensitive" sort of guy, he feels reasonably good about his choices because he is spending so much more time with his son Jeff than did Rick's father with him. By contrast, Joanie feels that she is not doing right by either of her identities—that she is shortchanging her roles as both parent and professional.

Children need both quality and quantity time. And, they can easily consume all of the time and energy that parents are willing to commit. Will you find it acceptable to limit your parenting to the time and energy left over from work? And, what will be the reactions of your children to this ordering of priorities?

Children also provide us with many wonderful opportunities to share in their lives and experience great enjoyment. Are you going to be satisfied missing your daughter's soccer game or your son's gymnastics meet? Are you going to be satisfied not being able to chaperone your daughter's school trip or take your son trick-or-treating?

In THE WASHINGTONIAN article discussed at the beginning of this chapter, Guberman quoted a soon-to-retire "big-firm partner":

> "See those trinkets?" He points to a shelf lined with glass-encased corporate icons and other memorabilia clients have given him. "Each of those reminds me of another slice of my family's life that went to pot because I had to stay holed up at work."

Will you be in a similar position to that partner at the end of your legal career, looking back sadly at the lost moments with family? Will you be satisfied remembering the evenings of missed family dinners and coming home after the children were put to bed? It is better to confront those tradeoffs now than to look back in the future when these choices are too late to undo.

Many work settings do not provide much support for parents wanting to give their children all that they deserve. Even in those settings where lip service is paid to the importance of balancing personal and professional lives, lawyers who take time out to be with their children may be viewed as less serious and less committed to the work setting and to their careers.

Having children and being a parent are not important to all persons. However, if being a "good" parent is important to you, you will need to look for a work setting that really supports that choice. Otherwise, the tensions between professional expectations and personal obligations will prove to be untenable and will literally make you crazy. To avoid that outcome, you need to be conscious of this potential conflict and to look for a setting that will provide you with the kind of freedom that you need to be the kind of parent you want to be. But, like every other choice, there will be tradeoffs that must be embraced.

E. Making the Choices

In the musical *Rent*, there is a theme that runs throughout the show. The song "Seasons of Love" is sung by the cast after one of the characters succumbs to AIDS. In self-reflection, the characters ask, "How do you measure the life of a woman or man?" What we need to do as lawyers and as human beings is to make the choices that will allow us to answer that question in ways that are true to ourselves and our constellation of needs and beliefs.

In clinic, you began to learn about the aspects of lawyering that will let you positively sum up your life in this profession. You also were forced to balance, at least to some extent, your professional and personal lives and to make choices that will help guide you in the future. The goal, we hope, is that you will forge a career that reflects the kinds of choices that will allow you to proudly measure your life as a woman or man.

You are not entering the only profession in which choices must be made. However, the range of opportunities within the law is at least as great as that available in other careers. Knowing what you need to feel good about yourself means that you can begin to look within that range of opportunities to find the work setting or settings that will give you what you need. And, more and more within the law, you will have the chance to make multiple career choices and to reinvent yourself numerous times as a lawyer.

You are also not entering the only profession in which participants are often damaged by their choices. Substance dependencies, stress and other disorders, relationship dysfunction, and other disabilities are among the forms of injury that are not only too common among lawyers, but also among other professionals. This chapter is meant as an opportunity to reduce the likelihood that you will be a casualty. Being a lawyer can be a wonderful career. However, achieving a wonderful career requires being honest with yourself and making choices and accepting tradeoffs consistent with your needs and your goals.

Index